Learning
MANDARIN
CHINESE
CHARACTERS

VOLUME 2

YI REN

TUTTLE Publishing

Tokyo │ Rutland, Vermont │ Singapore

I would like to dedicate this book to my children:
Lillian, Sandra and Justinian

Published by Tuttle Publishing, an imprint of Periplus Editions (HK) Ltd

www.tuttlepublishing.com

Copyright © 2017 Periplus Editions (HK) Ltd
Front cover photo © takayuki/Shutterstock.com
Photo page 6: Wikimedia Commons

ISBN: 978-0-8048-4494-9

Distributed by

North America, Latin America & Europe
Tuttle Publishing
364 Innovation Drive
North Clarendon,
VT 05759-9436 U.S.A.
Tel: 1 (802) 773-8930
Fax: 1 (802) 773-6993
info@tuttlepublishing.com
www.tuttlepublishing.com

Asia Pacific
Berkeley Books Pte. Ltd.
61 Tai Seng Avenue, #02-12
Singapore 534167
Tel: (65) 6280-1330
Fax: (65) 6280-6290
inquiries@periplus.com.sg

20 19 18 17   10 9 8 7 6 5 4 3 2 1

Printed in Singapore   1701MP

Contents

Some Tips on Learning Mandarin Chinese Characters

Look at the nature surrounding you, the mountains, the rivers, the trees, the flowers, the animals and the people. All have different shapes and different voices. Ancient Chinese people living within this beautiful world found a unique way for humans to communicate with each other. They created Chinese characters!

From oracle-bone script to bronze inscriptions, from seal script to clerical script, from regular script to simplified Chinese characters, centuries upon centuries have passed by and those square shaped figures are still being used by a vast population today.

Ancient Modern Ancient Modern

	Ancient	Modern		Ancient	Modern	
Tortoise						Bright
Above						Moon
Hill						Below
Stag						Bird
Eye						Ear
Forest						Man

Chinese characters from past to present

There are two other ancient writing systems known to man, the Sumerian cuneiform and the Egyptian hieroglyphs. Of the three, the Chinese character writing system is the only ancient writing system still being used today. Credit for this goes to several distinct features that make Chinese characters unique.

Three Basic Elements of the Chinese Character: Form, Sound and Meaning
汉字的三个基本要素: 形,音,义

Chinese characters are known as square shaped characters. Each character is made up of three basic elements: form, sound and meaning. For example,

"我" is the form.
"**wǒ**" is the sound.
"I" is the meaning.

Over time, there have been many changes in the phonetics of Chinese characters. The composition and meanings, however, have remained somewhat the same. As a result, many Chinese speaking people today can read ancient texts without much difficulty.

Before the inception of Chinese characters, communication was difficult within China due to the number of vastly different dialects being spoken. Chinese characters gave people a common ground for understanding.

One Syllable and Single Characters
单音节和独体字

Chinese characters are single characters with one syllable. These characters are created by drawing pictures of objects. Over time the characters have evolved from pictures into symbols. The symbols were standardized, then simplified to make writing easier. This simplified version is very basic in structure. It can't be divided into components or radicals. For example,

月 **yuè** means "moon"
木 **mù** means "tree" or "wood"
山 **shān** means "mountain"
水 **shuǐ** means "water"

Many of these types of characters are classified as Chinese "pictograms. "

In addition, there is another small category of characters that are direct iconic illustrations. Examples of these include:

上 **shàng** for "up" and 下 **xià** for "down".

These were originally a dot above and below a line. Single number characters, such as,

一 **yī** for "one"
二 **èr** for "two"
三 **sān** for "three"

are also included in this category.

Composed Characters with New Meanings
具有新义的合体字

In the Chinese language there are many compound characters. Compound characters are made up of two or more single characters. When single characters are joined, the meaning and pronunciation of the character can change dramatically. There are twelve ways to compose Chinese characters. For example,

from top to bottom: 日 + 生 = 星
from left to right: 其 + 月 = 期
from left to middle to right:
言(讠) + 身 + 寸 = 谢 and so on.

Here are two frequently used ways to compose compound characters.

1) Two single characters may be combined to create a new single character with a new meaning.

木	+	交	➡	校
wood		cross, hand over		school

女	+	子	➡	好
woman		son, seed		good

2) Two single characters may be joined to form a new word. This new word is pronounced by speaking the individual characters, one after the other. The definition of this newly formed word may be similar to the individual original definitions or it may be completely changed. Look carefully at the following examples.

飞	+	机	➡	飞机
fly		machine, plane		plane, aircraft
读	+	书	➡	读书
read		book		read book
关	+	系	➡	关系
close, shut		system, series		relationship

In this book, you will see that many compound characters are composed in these two ways.

Various Radicals   多样化的偏旁部首

A Chinese radical (or "section header") is sometimes considered a "classifier." It is a particular component of most compound characters that can be found in various positions within the word. The radical usually gives a clue as to the meaning of the character. It can also help with the pronunciation of a word. Characters with the same radical can be grouped together for the easy of studying or used as a point of reference for indexing. The Chinese dictionary is a great example of this.

As you look through this book, you will find that Chinese characters, such as 吗, 吃, 妈, 她, the 口 and 女 are called radicals. You may wonder how or why a single character, such as 口 or 女, can become a radical. The answer is this: When compound characters are composed of two single characters, one of those characters becomes the radical. You can see it here in 吗, 吃, 妈, and 她.

Radicals, such as 口 and 女 keep their original single character form, but their shape may be narrowed or shortened. Many character components are distorted or changed in order to fit within the block shape alongside other characters. Some words or characters may take on a different shape completely. For example,

人 turns to 亻 as a radical for 你, 他, and 们.
言 changes to 讠 as a radical for 说, 话, and 读.
水 becomes 氵 as a radical for 沙, 河, and 湖.

These are only a few examples to give you a general idea.

For many years, Chinese dictionaries have contained more than 200 radicals. You will easily be able to memorize the list of commonly used radicals offered here. They appear often in this book.

Some Commonly Used Chinese Radicals

Radicals 偏旁部首	Examples 字例	Radicals 偏旁部首	Examples 字例
亻	你，他，们	宀	家，字，宝
女	妈，姐，她	口	吃，喝，唱
讠	说，话，语	日	明，昨，晴
氵	汉，河，漂	阝	那，都，院
纟	红，绿，纱	辶	这，边，还
木	样，校，椅	艹	茶，草，菜

Chinese radicals appear in various positions within the word or character. Some radicals appear on the left side of the character 你，他，们, while other radicals appear on the right side of the character 都，那，邓. Some radicals appear at the top of a character 茶，菜，花, while other radicals appear at the bottom of a character 名，合，右. In general, semantic components tend to appear at the top or on the left side of character, while phonetic components tend to appear at the bottom or on the right side of character. As you learn more Chinese characters, you will learn to recognize the radicals in their various positions. Recognizing the radicals will also help you increase your vocabulary quickly.

The Strokes of Chinese Characters
汉字的笔画

When you use a pencil, pen or brush to draw pictures, you draw lines, circles or curves, one step at a time. When you use a pencil, pen or brush to write Chinese characters, you make lines, dots or hooks, one step at a time. The principles for drawing pictures and writing Chinese characters are very much the same. Far from being complicated, Chinese characters are simple drawings made from simple strokes. There are about thirty strokes in all. Among them are eight basic strokes that form the core and are used most often. All strokes have their own name and particular method of formation.

See the table below containing the eight basic strokes and how to form them.

Eight Basic Strokes and Method of Formation

Stroke 笔画	Name 名称	Writing direction 书写方向	Writing instruction 写法要点	Examples 字例
一	horizontal stroke 横 / héng	written from left to right	horizontal with the right end slightly up	二
丨	vertical stroke 竖 / shù	written from top to bottom	straight from top to bottom	十
丿	downward-left stroke 撇 / piě	written from top right to bottom left	start with force, end slightly	人
乀	downward-right stroke 那 / nà	written from top left to bottom right	start with force, pull to the right in the end	大
丶	dot 点 / diǎn	written from top to bottom right or left	dot to lower right or left, then pause	学
⟋	upward stroke 提 / tí	written from bottom left to top right	to upper-right, thinner at the end	习
亅	hook stroke 勾 / gōu	vertical stroke with a hook	a vertical line with a tiny rising tip at the end	小
𠃌	turning stroke 折 / zhé	horizontal stroke with a vertical downturn	horizontal stroke, turn to the right down in vertical	口

Learn to recognize and become familiar with each individual stroke, its name, writing direction and correct formation are all important. Whether the character is simple or complex, comprised of just a few strokes or many, the construction of each Chinese character relies heavily upon correct stroke formation. By focusing on the individual strokes, you will also be memorizing the character.

Stroke Order and Rules
笔画顺序规则

Throughout the years, rules have developed for writing Chinese characters. These rules help in learning the correct formation of characters. It doesn't matter whether you are right handed or left handed. If you follow the rules for stroke order, you will be able to write beautiful Chinese characters.

Here are the main stroke order rules for forming Chinese characters. These general rules will help you to understand more specific stroke order rules later on.

1) Stroke from top to bottom

| 号 | number | page 11 |
| 票 | ticket | page 101 |

2) Stroke from left to right

| 但 | but | page 82 |
| 眼 | eye | page 108 |

3) Stroke from the horizontal before vertical

| 正 | positive | page 54 |
| 报 | report | page 99 |

4) Stroke from the horizontal before the down stroke to the left

| 左 | left | page 45 |
| 右 | right | page 45 |

5) Stroke from the down stroke to left before to the right

| 从 | from | page 72 |
| 服 | clothing | page 56 |

6) The enclosing strokes first, then the enclosed and finally the sealing stroke

| 因 | cause | page 62 |
| 国 | country | page 88 (Vol 1) |

7) The dot on the top or left first

| 弟 | younger brother | page 18 |
| 牛 | cow | page 26 |

8) Inside stroke before side stroke

| 远 | far | page 70 |
| 近 | near | page 70 |

Following these simple rules will help you write any character you desire. Just remember to form the strokes correctly and in the right order from the very start. Otherwise you will find yourself repeating the same mistakes without knowing it. Correct stroke formation and stroke order will become more critical as your Chinese characters become more complex.

The Philosophy of Writing Chinese Characters
书写汉字的哲学

What is the philosophy behind writing Chinese characters? The philosophy can be summed up in one simple word: Balance!

Balance means, the writer needs to remain calm in emotion and thought, focused on the character and follow the rules of stroke formation and stroke order. Remember to place the strokes evenly throughout left to right, top to bottom, outside to inside, inside to outside, etc.

Take a look at these characters:

山, 水 and 朋 are balanced from left to right;
早, 果 and 召 are balanced from and top to bottom;
国, 园 and 围 are balanced from outside to inside.

Each character appears to be accurate, well balanced and will look beautiful on paper.

Imagine drawing a person with a big head and small legs. Or a person with one arm longer than the other. The drawing would not look right. It would not look good. It might even look as though the picture could tip over or fall down. In any case, it would not look balanced. In that same way, if you write a character with longer strokes on the left and shorter strokes on the right, it won't look balanced either. It won't look accurate. It won't look good on paper. For example, look at the character 山—**shān**—"mountain." The center stroke is the longest, which represents the top of the mountain. Both sides contain vertical strokes which are the same in length. Thus, the character 山 is balanced. It looks accurate. It looks good on paper. If the left vertical stroke were longer than the right vertical stroke, the 山—mountain may appear off center or off balance. It may look as though the mountain could crumble to the ground.

In short, keep this simple word in mind when writing Chinese characters: "Balance!"

Enjoy Your Handwriting
祝你愉快地学写汉字

The same philosophy is true for both daily life and writing Chinese letters. Balance is the key. I kept this in mind while designing this book. This book is for all people everywhere and at all levels. It can be used by youth or students who want to learn and practice writing Chinese characters on their own. It can also be used by people who are preparing to take the HSK Level 2 exam and as a foundation of AP Chinese exam. The characters and composed words are chosen from the HSK Level 2 exam. These characters and words are essential for studying the Chinese language. (The HSK exam is a Chinese Proficiency Test or Chinese Standard Exam for all non-Chinese speakers. The HSK exam is similar to the TOEFL exam for non-English speakers. The difference between the two is, the HSK exam has six test levels.)

Once you begin work in this book, you will find that following the step by step stroke order makes writing Chinese characters simple and easy. Use the space provided to practice writing on your own. In addition to writing individual characters, you will soon be able to write composed words and complete the practice exercises.

Each practice exercise is designed to reinforce, as well as extend, the learner's knowledge. You will quickly become very familiar with the vast number of Chinese characters offered here. You will know how to form Chinese characters use them properly. There are twelve exercises in all. Each practice exercise is a culmination of material covered. For your convenience, an "Answer Key" is provided in the back of the book.

On each page with a featured Chinese character, you will find step by step stroke order directions which are easy to follow. You will also find three vocabulary words, phrases or idioms which relate to that featured Chinese character. Those phrases, idioms and proverbs are particularly well known in China and used in written, as well as oral language.

An index with English, Chinese characters and Pinyin is also provided in the back of this book. It is arranged in alphabetical order, making it easier for English speakers to search for Chinese characters.

As previously mentioned, all characters in this book are written in the simplified Chinese style. This is due to the fact that most people use this format. Today, Chinese writing is horizontal and moves from left to right, as in English. But in the past, Chinese writing was vertical and went from top to bottom, right to left.

As in art, you will find a sense of joy and accomplishment in creating beautiful Chinese characters. As you look at the characters you created with your own hand, you will be motivated to write even more. This process of handwriting stimulates many parts of your brain. It improves your memory, as well as your creativity. I truly hope that you find the practice of writing Chinese characters a joyous and rewarding experience.

Yi Ren

I would like to express my appreciation to my editor, June Chong, for her professional advice in creating this book; to my friend Karen Enos for her proof-reading and editorial suggestions; to my friend Yang-yang Li who helped make the index for this book; to my husband Suisheng Zhao and our children Lillian, Sandra and Justinian who have always supported me. Thank you all for your help with this project!

| 号 (5 strokes) | **hào** number, size, date 號 Traditional | **common words** 号码 **hàomǎ** number 号召 **hàozhào** to call; to appeal 发号施令 **fā hào shī lìng** (idiom) to boss people around | **radical** 口 |

| 丨 | 口 | 吕 | 呂 | 号 | 号 | 号 | 号 | | |

| 快 (7 strokes) | **kuài** fast, quickly, hurry up | **common words** 快件 **kuàijiàn** express mail 快车 **kuàichē** express train or bus 快人快语 **kuài rén kuài yǔ** (idiom) straight talk from an honest person; quick decision | **radical** 忄 |

| 丨 | 丷 | 忄 | 忄 | 忄 | 快 | 快 | 快 | 快 | |

| 乐 (5 strokes) | **lè** happy, cheerful **yuè** music 樂 Traditional | **common words** 快乐 **kuàilè** happy 音乐 **yīnyuè** music 乐极生悲 **lè jí shēng bēi** (idiom) extreme joy turns to sorrow | **radical** 丿 |

| 一 | 乍 | 乐 | 乐 | 乐 | 乐 | 乐 | 乐 | | |

| 迎 (7 strokes) | **yíng** welcome, greet | **common words** 欢迎 **huānyíng** welcome
迎合 **yínghé** to cater to; to pander to
迎刃而解 **yíng rèn ér jiě** (lit.) splits when it meets the knife's edge; (fig.) easily solved | **radical** 辶 |

| 始 (8 strokes) | **shǐ** begin, start | **common words** 开始 **kāishǐ** start; begin
始末 **shǐmò** beginning and end; whole story
始终不渝 **shǐzhōng bùyú** consistent; steadfast | **radical** 女 |

| 介 (4 strokes) | **jiè** introduce, between | **common words** 介绍 **jièshào** introduction; to introduce
介入 **jièrù** to intervene; to get involved
一介书生 **yī jiè shūshēng** be nothing but a scholar; an intellectual | **radical** 人 |

送

sòng
send off,
deliver,
give

(9 strokes)

common words

送货　**sònghuò**　deliver goods
送客　**sòngkè**　see a visitor out
送往迎来　**sòngwǎng yínglái**　bid farewell
to those departing and greet the arrival of
newcomers

radical
辶

给

gěi
give,
by,
for

給
Traditional

(9 strokes)

common words

给予　**gěiyǔ**　give
给力　**gěilì**　to put in extra effort
给以　**gěiyǐ**　to grant; to give

radical
纟

您

nín
you (polite)

(11 strokes)

common words

您好　**nínhǎo**　hello (polite)
您早　**nínzǎo**　good morning
您们　**nínmen**　you (plural)

radical
心

| 贵 (9 strokes) | **guì** honorable, expensive, valuable 貴 Traditional | **common words** 贵客 **guìkè** distinguished guest 贵族 **guìzú** noble; aristocrat 贵人多忘事 **guìrén duō wàngshì** (lit.) a man of distinction always has a poor memory | **radical** 贝 |

| 虫 | 虫 | 虫 | 虫 | 贵 | 贵 | 贵 | 贵 | 贵 | 贵 | 贵 |

| 贵 | | | | | | | | | | |

| | | | | | | | | | | |

| 姓 (8 strokes) | **xìng** one's family name | **common words** 姓名 **xìngmíng** full name 姓氏 **xìngshì** surname 尊姓大名 **zūnxìng dàmíng** May I know your name? | **radical** 女 |

| 乀 | 女 | 女 | 女 | 妙 | 妙 | 姓 | 姓 | 姓 | 姓 | 姓 |

| | | | | | | | | | | |

| | | | | | | | | | | |

| 最 (12 strokes) | **zuì** most | **common words** 最好 **zuìhǎo** the best 最多 **zuìduō** maximum 最终 **zuìzhōng** final; ultimate | **radical** 日 |

| 冖 | 曰 | 曰 | 旦 | 旦 | 冐 | 冐 | 冐 | 冐 | 冐 | 最 |

| 最 | 最 | 最 | 最 | | | | | | | |

| | | | | | | | | | | |

WORD PRACTICE

生日 **shēngrì** birthday

生	日								

快乐 **kuàilè** happy

快	乐								

欢迎 **huānyíng** welcome

欢	迎								

大家 **dàjiā** everyone, big family

大	家								

开始 **kāishǐ** start, begin

开	始								

介绍 **jièshào** introduce

介	绍								

EXERCISE SET 1 • 练习一
Happy Birthday • 祝你生日快乐

1. Choose the correct words from the boxes to complete the sentence.

欢迎	快乐	介绍	大家	贵姓	开始

1) 新的一天（　　　　　）了。

2) （　　　　　）你来中国！

3) 我们（　　　　　）都很高兴认识你！

4) 请问，您（　　　　　）？

5) 我来给你（　　　　　）一下我的朋友。

6) 祝你生日（　　　　　）！

2. Identify the characters with the same radical. Then write the characters in the space provide.

绍	送	姓	迎	最
星	始	给	她	这

辶: _____, _____, _____   纟: _____, _____

日: _____, _____   女: _____, _____. _____

3. Read the dialog. Answer the questions using Chinese characters.

(Q: question   A: answer)

1)   小明: 今天是十月六号，星期五，是我的生日。
      东东: 祝你生日快乐！
      Q: 小明的生日是几月几号？星期几？

      A: _____

2)   东东: 你爸爸会送给你什么东西？
      小明: 他要送我一本我最喜欢的书。
      Q: 小明的爸爸要送给他什么东西？

      A: _____

3)   小明: 你开始学中文了吗？
      东东: 还没有，明年我要去中国学中文。
      Q: 东东要去哪儿学中文？什么时候？

      A: _____

4)   小明: 今天是我生日，也是我最快乐的一天！
      东东: 我也为你高兴。祝你生日快乐！
      Q: 为什么今天是小明最快乐的一天？

      A: _____

| 哥
(10 strokes) | **gē**
older brother | **common words**
哥哥　**gēge**　older brother
大哥　**dàgē**　the eldest of one's brothers
哥伦比亚　**gē lún bǐ yà**　Colombia | radical
一 |

一	丌	丙	可	可	丙	哥	哥	哥	哥	哥
哥	哥									

| 弟
(7 strokes) | **dì**
younger brother | **common words**
弟弟　**dìdi**　younger brother
弟妹　**dìmèi**　sister-in-law (younger brother's wife)
兄弟姐妹　**xiōngdì jiěmèi**　brothers and sisters | radical
丷 |

丶	丷	当	当	肖	弟	弟	弟	弟	弟	

| 妹
(8 strokes) | **mèi**
younger sister | **common words**
妹妹　**mèimei**　younger sister
妹夫　**mèifū**　brother-in law (younger sister's husband)
姐妹　**jiěmèi**　sisters | radical
女 |

乚	女	女	女	女	奸	妹	妹	妹	妹	妹

| 丈 (3 strokes) | **zhàng** husband, a measurement unit | **common words** 丈量 **zhàngliàng** to measure 丈夫 **zhàngfū** husband 丈母娘 **zhàng mǔ niáng** mother-in law (wife's mother) | **radical** 一 |

| 一 | 丆 | 丈 | 丈 | 丈 | 丈 | | | | |

| 妻 (8 strokes) | **qī** wife | **common words** 妻子 **qīzi** wife 妻小 **qīxiǎo** wife and children 妻离子散 **qī lí zǐ sàn** (idiom) a family wrenched apart | **radical** 女 |

| 一 | 二 | 丰 | 丰 | 妻 | 妻 | 妻 | 妻 | 妻 | 妻 | 妻 |

| 孩 (9 strokes) | **hái** child | **common words** 孩提 **háití** early childhood; infancy 孩子 **háizi** child; children 孩子气 **háizǐ qì** childish | **radical** 子 |

| 了 | 了 | 孑 | 孑 | 孖 | 孩 | 孩 | 孩 | 孩 | 孩 |
| 孩 | | | | | | | | | |

男	**nán** man, male	**common words**		radical
(7 strokes)		男人　**nánrén**　man; male 男士　**nánshì**　man; gentleman 男耕女织　**nángēng nǔzhī**　(idiom) men plough the fields and women weave		田

丿｜ 冂日 冂日 田 田 男 男 男 男 男

常	**cháng** often, normal	**common words**		radical
(11 strokes)		非常　**fēicháng**　very; extraordinary 常客　**chángkè**　frequent visitor 常来常往　**chánglái chángwǎng**　to visit frequently; to see each other often		巾

丨 ⺍ ⺌ ⺌ 常 常 常 常 常 常 常

常 常 常

玩	**wán** to play	**common words**		radical
(8 strokes)		玩具　**wánjù**　toy 玩笑　**wánxiào**　joke 玩物丧志　**wánwù sàngzhì**　(idiom) infatuation with fine details prevents one making progress		王

二 三 王 王 玗 玗 玩 玩 玩 玩

笑 (10 strokes)	**xiào** smile, laugh	**common words** 笑容　**xiàoróng**　a smiling expression 笑纳　**xiàonà**　to kindly accept (an offering) 笑话百出　**xiàohuà bǎi chū**　make many 　　　　 ridiculous mistakes	**radical** 竹

ノ	片	生	绐	竹	竹	竿	竺	竿	笑	笑
笑	笑									

房 (8 strokes)	**fáng** house, room	**common words** 房东　**fángdōng**　landlord 房间　**fángjiān**　room 房地产　**fáng dìchǎn**　real estate	**radical** 户

`	二	三	户	户	户	房	房	房	房	房

WORD PRACTICE

哥哥 **gēge** older brother

哥	哥								

姐姐 **jiějie** older sister

姐	姐								

弟弟 **dìdi** younger brother

弟	弟								

妹妹 **mèimei** younger sister

妹	妹								

丈夫 **zhàngfū** husband

丈	夫								

妻子　**qīzi**　wife

妻	子							

孩子　**háizi**　child, children

孩	子							

男人　**nánrén**　man, male

男	人							

女人　**nǚrén**　woman, female

女	人							

房间　**fángjiān**　room

房	间							

非常　**fēicháng**　very, extraordinary

非	常							

1. **Add Pinyin and English next to the Chinese characters.**

丈夫 (_____ , _____)　　妻子 (_____ , _____)

男人 (_____ , _____)　　女人 (_____ , _____)

哥哥 (_____ , _____)　　弟弟 (_____ , _____)

姐姐 (_____ , _____)　　妹妹 (_____ , _____)

孩子 (_____ , _____)　　房间 (_____ , _____)

2. **Choose correct words from the box to complete each sentence.**

北京	妻子	常常	电视	电影	玩笑	在一起	丈夫

1)　我们一家人 (　　　) 喜欢在一起看 (　　　) 和
　　(　　　) 。

2)　我的哥哥和姐姐在 (　　　) 工作。

3)　我们常常 (　　　) 吃饭和说笑话。

4)　我的 (　　　) 是一个很好的女人。

5)　她的 (　　　) 也是一个很好的男人。

6)　我的儿子最喜欢开 (　　　) 。

3. Make your own sentences using the characters provided.

Example: 非常：我非常喜欢看电影。

1) 一起　：＿＿＿＿＿＿＿＿＿＿＿＿＿＿＿＿＿＿＿＿

2) 开玩笑：＿＿＿＿＿＿＿＿＿＿＿＿＿＿＿＿＿＿＿＿

3) 姐妹　：＿＿＿＿＿＿＿＿＿＿＿＿＿＿＿＿＿＿＿＿

4. Read the paragraph. Answer the questions using Chinese characters.

我叫李星。这是我的家人。那是我家的房子。这是我的丈夫，他是医生，在医院工作。这是我的三个孩子。这是我的大儿子，二十一岁，在上大学；这是小儿子，十七岁，在上高中；女儿十二岁，在上中学。我是老师，在中学工作。

1) 李星的丈夫做什么工作？

＿＿＿＿＿＿＿＿＿＿＿＿＿＿＿＿＿＿＿＿＿＿＿

2) 李星做什么工作？

＿＿＿＿＿＿＿＿＿＿＿＿＿＿＿＿＿＿＿＿＿＿＿

3) 李星的大儿子多大，在做什么？小儿子呢？

＿＿＿＿＿＿＿＿＿＿＿＿＿＿＿＿＿＿＿＿＿＿＿

＿＿＿＿＿＿＿＿＿＿＿＿＿＿＿＿＿＿＿＿＿＿＿

4) 李星的女儿多大，也在上学吗？

＿＿＿＿＿＿＿＿＿＿＿＿＿＿＿＿＿＿＿＿＿＿＿

| 鱼
(8 strokes) | **yú**
fish

魚
Traditional | **common words**
鱼油　**yúyóu**　fish oil
鱼片　**yúpiàn**　sliced fish meat
鱼水情深　**yúshuǐ qíngshēn**　close relation-
　　ship as between fish and water | radical
鱼 |

ノ	ク	个	鱼	鱼	鱼	鱼	鱼	鱼	鱼	鱼

| 羊
(6 strokes) | **yáng**
lamb,
sheep | **common words**
羊毛　**yángmáo**　wool
羊皮　**yángpí**　sheep skin
羊肉　**yángròu**　lamb meat; mutton | radical
羊 |

ヽ	ソ	兰	兰	兰	羊	羊	羊	羊		

| 牛
(4 strokes) | **niú**
cow | **common words**
牛排　**niúpái**　steak
牛奶　**niúnǎi**　milk
多如牛毛　**duō rú niúmáo**　(lit.) as many as
　　the hairs on an ox; countless; innumerable | radical
牛 |

ノ	⺧	乍	牛	牛	牛	牛				

| 鸡 (7 strokes) | jī chicken 雞 Traditional | **common words** 鸡腿 **jītuǐ** chicken leg 鸡胸 **jīxiōng** chicken breast 鸡蛋 **jīdàn** (chicken) egg | radical 鸟 |

| フ | 又 | 又 | 叉 | 鸡 | 鸡 | 鸡 | 鸡 | 鸡 | 鸡 | |

| 咖 (8 strokes) | kā coffee gā curry | **common words** 咖啡 **kāfēi** coffee 咖喱 **gālí** curry 咖啡馆 **kāfēiguǎn** coffee house; café | radical 口 |

| 丨 | 口 | 口 | 叮 | 叻 | 叻 | 咖 | 咖 | 咖 | 咖 | 咖 |

| 瓜 (5 strokes) | guā melon | **common words** 瓜子 **guāzǐ** melon seeds 西瓜 **xīguā** watermelon 瓜熟蒂落 **guā shú dì luò** (idiom) when the melon is ripe, it falls; problems sort themselves out in due time | radical 瓜 |

| 一 | 厂 | 厂 | 瓜 | 瓜 | 瓜 | 瓜 | 瓜 | | | |

已	**yǐ** already, then	**common words**	radical
(3 strokes)		已往　**yǐwǎng**　in the past 已经　**yǐjīng**　already 为时已晚　**wéishí yǐwǎn**　already too late	己

⁷コ	²ヨ	³已	已	已	已

也	**yě** also, too, as well	**common words**	radical
(3 strokes)		也许　**yěxǔ**　perhaps 也好　**yěhǎo**　may as well 何其毒也　**hé qí dú yě**　(idiom) How 　　pernicious!; How poisonous!	乙

⁷乛	²也	³也	也	也	也

要	**yào** will, desire, to ask for **yāo** to request	**common words**	radical
(9 strokes)		要员　**yàoyuán**　important official 要求　**yāoqiú**　request; ask 要言不烦　**yàoyán bùfán**　to explain in simple 　　terms; succinct; concise	西

¹一	²厂	³両	⁴西	⁵西	⁶覀	⁷要	⁸要	⁹要	要
要									

28

还 hái
still, also, yet

(7 strokes)

還 Traditional

common words

还好 **háihǎo** not bad; tolerable; fortunately
还是 **háishì** still; or; nevertheless
还可以 **hái kěyǐ** alright; acceptable

radical 辶

完 wán
finish, whole, complete

(7 strokes)

common words

完成 **wánchéng** finish; accomplish
完全 **wánquán** entirely; complete
完美无缺 **wánměi wúquē** perfect and without blemish; flawless

radical 宀

真 zhēn
real, true, genuine

(10 strokes)

common words

真诚 **zhēnchéng** sincere; genuine
真相 **zhēnxiàng** the actual facts
真知灼见 **zhēnzhī zhuójiàn** deep (penetrating) insight

radical 八

WORD PRACTICE

羊肉 **yángròu** lamb meat, mutton

羊	肉								

牛奶 **niúnǎi** milk

牛	奶								

鸡蛋 **jīdàn** egg

鸡	蛋								

咖啡 **kāfēi** coffee

咖	啡								

西瓜 **xīguā** watermelon

西	瓜								

好吃 **hǎochī** tasty, delicious

好	吃								

已经 **yǐjīng** already

已	经								

也好 **yěhǎo** may as well

也	好								

EXERCISE SET 3 • 练习三
What Do You Like to Eat? • 你喜欢吃什么？

1. Rewrite these English words into Chinese characters.

fish (   )   mutton (   )

milk (   )   egg (   )

coffee (   )   tea (   )

watermelon (   )   apple (   )

2. Choose the words in the boxes to complete each sentence.

鸡蛋	经常	羊肉	咖啡	还要
吃饭	茶	鱼	牛肉	非常

1)   妈妈买了很多 _____ (mutton) 和 _____ (beef)。

2)   我们一家人非常喜欢吃 _____ (fish)。

3)   我们 _____ (often) 去饭馆 _____ (to eat)。

4)   这里的 _____ (coffee) 真好喝。

5)   你喜欢喝咖啡还是 _____ (tea)？

6)   你 _____ (still want) 吃点什么？

7)   那个 _____ (egg) 很大。

8)   我的哥哥 _____ (extremely) 喜欢看电影。

3. Create your own sentences using the characters provided.

Example: 常常：妈妈常常去那家商店买东西。

1)   还有：_____

2)   还要：_____

3)   经常：_____

4)   非常：_____

4. Read the questions. Write the answers using Chinese characters.

1)   我们去商店买了很多牛肉和羊肉。

   Q: 他们去商店买了什么东西？

   A: _____

       _____

2)   我们还买了鸡蛋，牛奶和很多菜。

   Q: 他们还买了什么东西？

   A: _____

       _____

3)   那家咖啡馆里也卖茶。

   Q: 那家咖啡馆里也卖什么？

   A: _____

       _____

4)　　我和妹妹都非常喜欢吃西瓜和苹果。

　　Q:　他们都非常喜欢吃什么？

　　A:　_____

　　　　_____

5. Observe the differences in each pair of phrases. Rewrite them in Chinese.

A1.　非常好　_____　　A2.　真好　_____

B1.　非常高兴_____　　B2.　真高兴_____

C1.　非常喜欢_____　　C2.　真喜欢_____

D1.　非常好看_____　　D2.　真好看_____

E1.　非常好吃_____　　E2.　真好吃_____

F1.　非常好喝_____　　F2.　真好喝_____

6. Fill in the space with the appropriate word choices.

买了	羊	商店	东西	牛
鸡	西瓜	也买了	咖啡店	茶
一杯	咖啡	非常	还会去	奶

星期天下午，妈妈和我去（　　　　　）买肉，

菜和水果。我们买了（　　　　　）肉，（　　　　　）

肉，（　　　　　）蛋和鱼。我们（　　　　　）很多

菜和牛（　　　　　　　）。我们还（　　　　　　　）苹果和

（　　　　　　　）。买完（　　　　　　　），妈妈和我去了一

家咖啡店。这家（　　　　　　　）的咖啡和茶都很好。 妈

妈要了一杯咖啡，我要了（　　　　　　　）茶。妈妈说她

的（　　　　　　　）很好喝，我的（　　　　　　　）也很好

喝。我们都（　　　　　　　）喜欢这家咖啡店，下次我们

（　　　　　　　）这家咖啡店喝咖啡和茶。

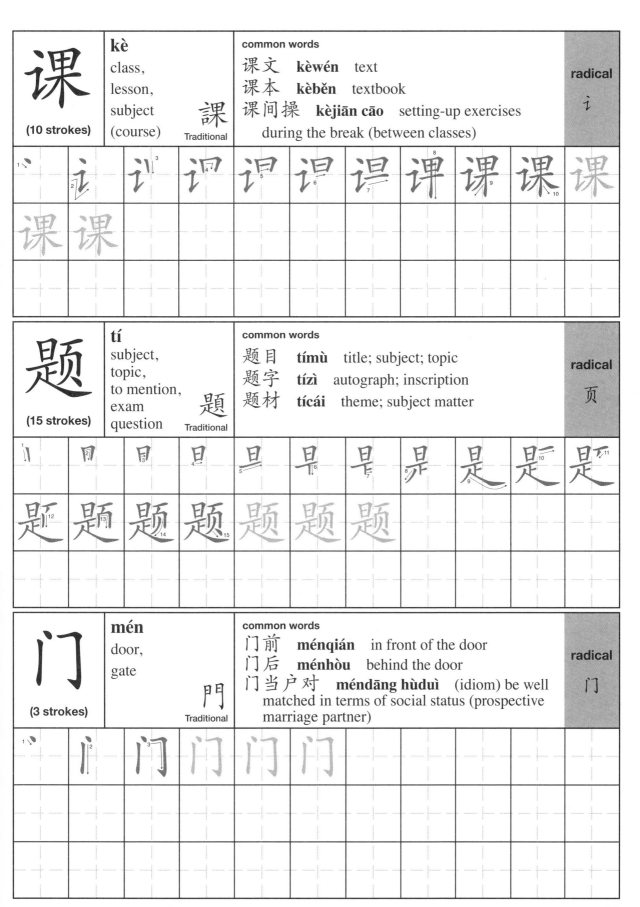

| 课 (10 strokes) | kè class, lesson, subject (course) | 課 Traditional | **common words** 课文 **kèwén** text 课本 **kèběn** textbook 课间操 **kèjiān cāo** setting-up exercises during the break (between classes) | radical 讠 |

| 题 (15 strokes) | tí subject, topic, to mention, exam question | 題 Traditional | **common words** 题目 **tímù** title; subject; topic 题字 **tízì** autograph; inscription 题材 **tícái** theme; subject matter | radical 页 |

| 门 (3 strokes) | mén door, gate | 門 Traditional | **common words** 门前 **ménqián** in front of the door 门后 **ménhòu** behind the door 门当户对 **méndāng hùduì** (idiom) be well matched in terms of social status (prospective marriage partner) | radical 门 |

考	**kǎo** to test, to examine	**common words** 考题 **kǎotí** exam question 考分 **kǎofēn** grade; exam mark 考试 **kǎoshì** exam; to take an exam	**radical** 耂
(6 strokes)			

一	十	土	少	考	考	考	考	考		

教	**jiāo/jiào** to teach, call, teaching	**common words** 教室 **jiàoshì** classroom 教师 **jiàoshī** teacher 教学相长 **jiàoxué xiāng zhǎng** when you teach someone, both teacher and student will benefit	**radical** 攵
(11 strokes)			

一	十	土	少	考	考	孝	孝	孝	教	教
教	教	教								

问	**wèn** to ask 問 Traditional	**common words** 问好 **wènhǎo** to send one's regards to 问题 **wèntí** question; problem 问长问短 **wèn cháng wèn duǎn** (idiom) take the trouble to make detailed inquiries	**radical** 门
(6 strokes)			

丶	门	门	问	问	问	问	问		

答	**dá** to answer, to respond, to reply	**common words**	
(12 strokes)		回答 **huídá** to reply; to answer 答案 **dáàn** answer; solution 答非所问 **dá fēi suǒ wèn** irrelevant answer	**radical** 竹

懂	**dǒng** understand, know	**common words**	
(15 strokes)		懂行 **dǒngháng** to know the ropes 懂得 **dǒngdé** understand; know; comprehend 不懂装懂 **bùdǒng zhuāngdǒng** to pretend to understand when you don't	**radical** 忄

错	**cuò** mistake, wrong	**common words**	
(13 strokes)	错 Traditional	错误 **cuòwù** mistake; error; 差错 **chācuò** mistake; slip-up; fault 错综复杂 **cuòzōng fùzá** (idiom) tangled and complicated	**radical** 钅

| 外 | wài
outside,
foreign,
in addition

(5 strokes) | **common words**
外交　**wàijiāo**　diplomacy; foreign affairs
外国　**wàiguó**　foreign country
外柔内刚　**wàiróu nèigāng**　(idiom) outwardly
　　　yielding but inwardly firm | radical
夕 |

ノ	夕	夕	外	外	外	外	外

| 知 | zhī
to know,
to be aware

(8 strokes) | **common words**
知道　**zhīdào**　to know; to become aware of
知名　**zhīmíng**　well-known; famous
知行合一　**zhīxíng héyī**　(idiom) the unity of
　　　knowledge and practice | radical
矢 |

ノ	仁	午	乍	矢	知	知	知	知	知	知

| 准 | zhǔn
allow,
standard,
accurate

(10 strokes)　準
　　　Traditional | **common words**
准时　**zhǔnshí**　on time; punctual
准确　**zhǔnquè**　exact; accurate
准备　**zhǔnbèi**　prepare; get ready | radical
冫 |

`	冫	冫	冫	冫	冫	冫	准	准	准
准	准								

| 帮
(9 strokes) | **bāng**
assist,
help,
gang | common words
帮忙　**bāngmáng**　help; lend a hand to
帮会　**bānghuì**　secret society; underworld gang
帮助　**bāngzhù**　help; assistance; aid | radical
巾 |

一	三	三	丰	邦	邦	帮	帮	帮	帮	帮
帮										

WORD PRACTICE

考试　**kǎoshì**　exam, test

考	试								

教室　**jiàoshì**　classroom

教	室								

问题　**wèntí**　question, problem

问	题								

回答　**huídá**　to answer, to reply

回	答								

知道　**zhīdào**　to know, be aware of

知	道								

准备 **zhǔnbèi** prepare, get ready

准	备								

帮助 **bāngzhù** help, assistance, aid

帮	助								

EXERCISE SET 4 • 练 习 四
In School • 在 学 校

1. **Add English and Pinyin with tones to each character. Pay particular attention to how the tones change the meaning of the word.**

Chinese Character	Pinyin	English	Chinese Character	Pinyin	English
教	jiāo	to teach	叫	jiào	call, to be called
字			子		
们			门		
没			妹		
羊			样		
完			玩		
非			飞		
买			卖		
前			钱		
机			鸡		
那			哪		

2. Write the correct Chinese characters to complete each sentence.

1) 那是我的 _____ (classroom)。

2) 今天我有四门 _____ (classes)。

3) 你知道怎样 _____ (answer) 那个问题吗？

4) 你能不能 _____ (help) 我？

3. Make your own sentences using the characters provided.

Example: 知道：你知道书店在哪里吗？

1) 回答：_____

2) 帮助：_____

3) 告诉：_____

4. Read the dialog. Answer the questions using Chinese characters.

1) 小明：你听懂老师说什么了吗？

东东：老师说得太快，我没有听懂。

小明：我也没听懂，我们去问问老师。

东东：好的，我们一起去。

Q: 东东为什么没有听懂？

A: _____

Q: 他们怎么办呢？

A: _____

2) 小明: 你弟弟的学校有两个外国学生，是吗？

   东东: 是的，你怎么知道的？。

   小明: 我听说的。他们会说汉语吗？

   东东: 他们的汉语很好，我们也很喜欢他们。

   Q: 东东弟弟的学校有几个外国学生？

   A: _____

   Q: 他们会说汉语吗？

   A: _____

3) 小明: 东东，你每天上几门课？

   东东: 我每天上五门课。

   小明: 一门课有多长时间？

   东东: 一门课是四十五分钟。

   Q: 东东每天上几门课？

   A: _____

   Q: 一门课有多长时间？

   A: _____

4) 小明： 东东，明天我们有三门考试，你准备好了吗？

东东： 还没有，你呢？

小明： 我准备好了。

东东： 我有一个问题做错了，我不知道怎么回答。

小明： 让我看看。这个题是这样回答，你懂了吗？

东东： 我懂了，谢谢你的帮助！

小明： 不客气！

Q: 他们什么时候有几门考试？

A: _____

Q: 他们准备好了吗？

A: _____

Q: 东东怎么没准备好？

A: _____

Q: 在小明的帮助下，东东懂了吗？

A: _____

找	**zhǎo**	**common words**	radical
(7 strokes)	to find, seek	找钱　**zhǎoqián**　to give charge 找到　**zhǎodào**　to find 找不自在　**zhǎo búzìzài**　to bring misfortune 　　　　upon oneself	扌

一　十　才　扌　扎　找　找　找　找　找

它	**tā**	**common words**	radical
(5 strokes)	it	它们　**tāmen**　they 它是　**tāshì**　it is 它有　**tāyǒu**　it has	宀

丶　宀　宀　它　它　它　它　它

可	**kě**	**common words**	radical
(5 strokes)	may, can, able to	可以　**kěyǐ**　can; may; possible 可能　**kěnéng**　probable; maybe; perhaps 可遇不可求　**kěyù bù kěqiú**　(idiom) can be 　　　　discovered but not sought	口

一　丁　可　可　可　可　可　可

向	**xiàng** towards, guide, direction	common words	
(6 strokes)		向左　**xiàngzuǒ**　leftwards; to the left 向上　**xiàngshàng**　upward 向隅而泣　**xiàngyú ér qì**　(idiom) to weep alone in a corner; be left to grieve in the cold	radical 口

向 向 向 向 向 向 向 向 向

左	**zuǒ** left	common words	
(5 strokes)		左边　**zuǒbiān**　the left side; to the left 左派　**zuǒpài**　the left wing (politics) 左思右想　**zuǒ sī yòu xiǎng**　to think through from different angles; to ponder	radical 工

左 左 左 左 左 左 左 左

右	**yòu** right	common words	
(5 strokes)		右边　**yòubiān**　the right side; to the right 右派　**yòupài**　the right wing (politics) 左右为难　**zuǒyòu wéinán**　in a dilemma; in a predicament	radical 口

右 右 右 右 右 右 右 右

旁 (10 strokes)	**páng** other, beside, one side	**common words** 旁人　**pángrén**　other people; bystanders 旁边　**pángbiān**　beside; to the side 旁观者清　**pángguānzhě qīng**　(idiom) the person on the spot is baffled, the spectator sees clear					radical 方
丶	二	六	立	立	产	产	产	旁	旁	旁
旁	旁						

进 (7 strokes)	**jìn** enter, advance 進 Traditional	**common words** 进入　**jìnrù**　to enter; to join; to go into 进步　**jìnbù**　progress 进退维谷　**jìntuì wéi gǔ**　(idiom) no room to advance or to retreat; trapped					radical 辶
一	二	丰	井	井	讲	进	进	进	进	

告 (7 strokes)	**gào** to tell, to say, to sue	**common words** 告别　**gàobié**　to leave; to bid farewell 告诉　**gàosù**　to inform; to tell 告老还乡　**gào lǎo huánxiāng**　retire and return to one's hometown					radical 口
丿	仁	牛	生	生	告	告	告	告	告	

左边 **zuǒbiān**   the left side, to the left

左	边							

右边 **yòubiān**   the right side, to the right

右	边							

旁边 **pángbiān**   beside, side

旁	边							

可以 **kěyǐ**   can, may, possible

可	以							

可能 **kěnéng**   probable, maybe, perhaps

可	能							

告诉 **gàosù**   to inform, to tell

告	诉							

1. Rewrite these directional words to become more familiar with them.

上面 _____   上边 _____

下面 _____   下边 _____

前面 _____   前边 _____

后面 _____   后边 _____

左面 _____   左边 _____

右面 _____   右边 _____

里面 _____   里边 _____

外面 _____   外边 _____

上上下下 _____   前前后后 _____

左左右右 _____   里里外外 _____

2. Read the questions. Answer the questions using Chinese characters.

1) 请问，商店在哪里？
The store is in the left side of the school.

_____

2) 你可以告诉我，医院在哪里吗？
The hospital is at back of that store.

_____

3) 火车站在哪儿？
The train station is on the right side of the hospital.

_____

4) 那家饭馆在商店的左边吗？
Yes, that restaurant is on the left side of the store.

_____

5) 外面天气怎么样？
The weather of outside is very good.

_____

6) 妈妈的茶杯在哪里？
Mother's cup is on the top of the table.

_____

7) 教室里面有很多学生吗？
Yes, there are many students in the classroom.

_____

8) 商店前面有很多车吗？

No, there are a few cars in the front of the store.

_____

3. **Make your own sentences using the characters provided.**

Example: 可以：你可以和我一起去书店吗？

1) 告诉 ：_____

2) 怎么去：_____

3) 前面 ：_____

4) 旁边 ：_____

4. **Read the paragraph. Answer the questions using Chinese characters.**

小明想去商店买点东西，可是，他不知道怎么去商店。他打电话问他的朋友，他朋友告诉他，那家商店的右边是一个火车站，左边是一家医院；商店的前面是一家书店，后面是一家很大的电影院。小明按照朋友说的方位，找到了那家商店。他买了他要的东西，很高兴。

1) 小明要去商店做什么？

_____

2) 小明不知道怎么去商店，怎么办？

_____

3) 火车站在商店的哪边？

_____

4) 医院在商店的哪边？

_____

5) 书店在商店的哪边？

_____

6) 电影院在商店的哪边？

_____

7) 小明为什么很高兴？

_____

| 颜 (15 strokes) | yán color, face 颜 Traditional | **common words** 颜料 **yánliào** coloring materials eg. dye, paint 颜色 **yánsè** color; countenance 颜面扫地 **yánmiàn sǎodì** (idiom) to be thoroughly discredited | radical 页 |

亠	二	六	立	立	产	产	彦	彦	彦	彦
颜	颜	颜	颜	颜	颜	颜				

| 红 (6 strokes) | hóng red (color) 红 Traditional | **common words** 红豆 **hóngdòu** red bean 红茶 **hóngchá** black tea 红光满面 **hóngguāng mǎnmiàn** a healthy and hearty look; glowing with health | radical 纟 |

乚	纟	纟	纟	红	红	红	红	红

| 白 (5 strokes) | bái white (color) | **common words** 白发 **báifà** white or gray hair 白宫 **báigōng** White House 白头偕老 **báitóu xiélǎo** remain happily married to a ripe old age; until death do us part | radical 白 |

丿	亻	冇	白	白	白	白	白

| 黑
(12 strokes) | **hēi**
black (color),
dark | **common words**
黑色　**hēisè**　black color
黑发　**hēifà**　black hair
黑灯瞎火　**hēi dēng xiā huǒ**　pitch dark | **radical**
黑 |

| 丶 | 口 | 冖 | 四 | 口 | 甲 | 罣 | 黑 | 罜 | 黑 | 黑 |

| 黑 | 黑 | 黑 | 黑 | | | | | | | |

| | | | | | | | | | | |

| 得
(11 strokes) | **dé**
gain,
get,
obtain | **common words**
得到　**dédào**　to get; to obtain; to receive
得奖　**déjiǎng**　to win a prize
觉得　**juéde**　to think; to feel | **radical**
彳 |

| 丿 | 彡 | 彳 | 彳 | 彳 | 彳 | 彳 | 彳 | 得 | 得 | 得 |

| 得 | 得 | 得 | | | | | | | | |

| | | | | | | | | | | |

| 穿
(9 strokes) | **chuān**
to wear,
to dress,
to put on | **common words**
穿过　**chuānguò**　to pass through
穿孔　**chuānkǒng**　punch a hole
穿针引线　**chuānzhēn yǐnxiàn**　(idiom) to
thread a needle; (fig.) to act as a go-between | **radical**
穴 |

| 丶 | 八 | 宀 | 宀 | 宀 | 空 | 空 | 穿 | 穿 | 穿 | |

| 穿 | | | | | | | | | | |

| | | | | | | | | | | |

53

件	**jiàn**	**common words**	radical
(6 strokes)	a measure word for things, item	信件　**xìnjiàn**　letter 条件　**tiáojiàn**　condition; prerequisite 一件衣服　**yījiàn yīfū**　a piece of clothing	亻

丿	亻	仁	作	仵	件	件	件	件		

张	**zhāng**	**common words**	radical
(7 strokes)	open, spread, a measure word for flat objects　张 **Traditional**	张开　**zhāngkāi**　to open up 张口　**zhāngkǒu**　to gape; to open one's mouth 张灯结彩　**zhāng dēng jiécǎi**　(idiom) to be decorated with lanterns and colored banners	弓

丁	弓	弓	引	引	张	张	张	张	张		

正	**zhèng**	**common words**	radical
(5 strokes)	main, positive, right	正在　**zhèngzài**　just at the right time 正常　**zhèngcháng**　normal; ordinary; regular 正确　**zhèngquè**　correct; proper	止

一	丁	下	止	正	正	正	正		

着 (11 strokes)	**zhe** a particle indicating action in progress	**common words** 看着 **kànzhe** to look at 接着 **jiēzhe** to continue; to carry on 看着不管 **kànzhe bùguǎn** to stand by and pay no heed; to ignore	**radical** 目

为 (4 strokes) 為 Traditional	**wèi** because of, for, to	**common words** 为了 **wèile** for the purpose of 为人 **wèirén** for somebody; for others' interest 为什么 **wèi shénme** why? for what reason?	**radical** 、

员 (7 strokes) 員 Traditional	**yuán** person, employee, member	**common words** 员工 **yuángōng** staff; employee 演员 **yǎnyuán** actor or actress; performer 服务员 **fúwù yuán** attendant; customer service personnel	**radical** 口

WORD PRACTICE

颜色 **yánsè** color

颜	色							

正在 **zhèngzài** just at the right time

正	在							

觉得 **juéde** to think, to feel

觉	得							

为什么 **wèi shénme** why?, for what reason?

为	什	么						

服务员 **fúwù yuán** attendant, customer service personnel

服	务	员						

EXERCISE SET 6 • 练习六
Colorful Clothing • 五颜六色的衣服

1. Add Pinyin and English next to the Chinese characters.

Chinese Characters	Pinyin	English	Chinese Characters	Pinyin	English
颜色			白色		
黑色			红色		
五颜六色			白色衣服		

2. Rewrite these phrases. Pay particular attention to how the underlined measure words are used.

一杯水 （　　　　　）　　　五件衣服 （　　　　　）

两杯茶 （　　　　　）　　　六个苹果 （　　　　　）

三本书 （　　　　　）　　　七张桌子 （　　　　　）

四块钱 （　　　　　）　　　八家医院 （　　　　　）

3. Rewrite these characters. Notice the differences in each pair of words.

zhēn　　zhèng

真 ➞ 正

zhēnpiàoliàng

真 漂 亮 （　　　　　） ➞

zhèngzài

正 在 （　　　　　）

jué   jiào

觉 —— 觉

juédé   shuìjiào

觉 得   (   ) ——► 睡 觉   (   )

jiàn   jiàn

件 ——► 见

yījiàn yīfū   zàijiàn

一 件 衣 服 (   ) ——► 再 见   (   )

4. Read the questions. Rewrite the answer using Chinese characters.

1)   你喜欢这件红色的衣服吗？
        I like this red clothing.

_____

2)   服务员，我可以试一试那件白色的上衣吗？
        Yes, you can try that white top.

_____

3)   这件衣服太大了，你们有小一点儿的吗？
        We don't have the small size.

_____

4)   这件衣服你穿着正好，买了吧！
        Okay, I'll buy this clothing.

_____

5)   这里有三个杯子，哪个是你的？
        That red color cup is mine.

_____

6) 你觉得这件黑色的衣服怎么样？

This black clothing is very beautiful.

_____

7) 你今天洗衣服了吗？

Yes, I washed my clothes today.

_____

8) 你最喜欢什么颜色？

My like the red color most.

_____

5. Make your own sentences using the characters provided.

   Example: 正好：现在正好是下午三点钟。

   1) 正在　　　：_____

   2) 觉得　　　：_____

   3) 试一试　　：_____

   4) 五颜六色：_____

6. Read the paragraph. Answer the questions using Chinese characters.

小明和东东去商店买衣服。小明看到了一件白色的上衣，他很喜欢。他问服务员可不可以试一试，服务员说："可以。"小明试穿了一下，告诉服务员"太大了"，服务员给了他一件小一点的衣服，小明穿上后，觉得正好，他就买了那件白上衣。东东呢，她喜欢那件红，黑和白三种颜色在一起的衣服，她试穿了一下，小明说："东东，你穿上这件衣服，真漂亮，快买了吧！"东东很高兴地买了那件衣服。

1)　　小明和东东去商店做什么？

_____

2)　　小明喜欢什么颜色的衣服？

_____

3)　　商店里的衣服可以试穿吗？

_____

4)　　小明为什么买了那件白上衣？

_____

5)　　东东喜欢什么颜色的衣服？

_____

6)　　东东也买了一件衣服，为什么？

_____

| 晴 (12 strokes) | **qíng** clear, sunny | **common words** 晴朗　**qínglǎng**　sunny and cloudless
晴好　**qínghǎo**　bright and sunny weather
晴空万里　**qíngkōng wànlǐ**　the vast clear sky | **radical** 日 |

| 阴 (6 strokes) | **yīn** cloudy, shady | **common words** 阴干　**yīngān**　dry in the shade
阴历　**yīnlì**　lunar calendar
阴差阳错　**yīnchā yángcuò**　(idiom) an accident arising from many causes | **radical** 阝 |

| 雪 (11 strokes) | **xuě** snow | **common words** 雪人　**xuěrén**　snowman
雪花　**xuěhuā**　snowflake
雪中送炭　**xuězhōng sòngtàn**　(lit.) to send charcoal in snowy weather; (fig.) timely assistance | **radical** 雨 |

因	**yīn** cause, reason	**common words** 因此　**yīncǐ**　therefore; as a result of 因果　**yīnguǒ**　course and effect; karma 因为　**yīnwèi**　because; owing to	**radical** 囗
(6 strokes)			

丨	冂	冂	囘	囙	因	因	因	因	

所	**suǒ** actually, place	**common words** 所有　**suǒyǒu**　to own; to possess 所以　**suǒyǐ**　therefore; as a result of 所向无前　**suǒ xiàng wú qián**　be invincible	**radical** 户
(8 strokes)			

'	厂	户	巨	戶	所	所	所	所	所	所

走	**zǒu** walk, go	**common words** 走红　**zǒuhóng**　to have good luck 走人　**zǒurén**　to leave; to go away 走马观花　**zǒumǎ guānhuā**　(lit.) flower 　　viewing on horseback; (fig.) superficial 　　understanding; a fleeting glance	**radical** 走
(7 strokes)			

一	十	土	丰	卡	走	走	走	走	走	

路	lù	common words	
(13 strokes)	road, journey, route	路口　**lùkǒu**　intersection (roads); crossing 路过　**lùguò**　passing by 一路平安　**yīlù píngān**　Have a safe journey!; 　　　　　　　　　　　Bon voyage!	radical 足

跑	pǎo	common words	
(12 strokes)	run, run away, escape	跑车　**pǎochē**　sports car 跑鞋　**pǎoxié**　running shoes 跑步　**pǎobù**　run; jog	radical 足

吧	ba	common words	
(7 strokes)	a particle, bar	走吧　**zǒuba**　let's go; let's leave 唱吧　**chàngba**　let's sing 酒吧　**jiǔba**　bar; pub	radical 口

WORD PRACTICE

因为 **yīnwèi** because, owing to

因	为									

所以 **suǒyǐ** therefore, as a result of

所	以									

走路 **zǒulù** to walk, to go on foot

走	路									

跑步 **pǎobù** to run

跑	步									

跑车 **pǎochē** sports car

跑	车									

1. Match the Chinese characters with their English and Pinyin partners.

晴	rain	**xuě**
阴	snow	**qíng**
雨	sunny	**lěng**
雪	cloudy	**yǔ**
风	hot	**yīn**
冷	wind	**rè**
热	cold	**fēng**

2. Rewrite these vocabulary. Notice the differences in usage for 在, 过, 了.

下雨（　　　）在下雨（　　　）下过雨了（　　　　　）

下雪（　　　）在下雪（　　　）下过雪了（　　　　　）

刮风（　　　）在刮风（　　　）刮风了　（　　　　　）

3. Rewrite these sentences. Become familiar with the usage of the words:

因为 ____ 所以____

1)　　因为天气太冷，所以我要多穿点衣服。

_____

2) 因为我喜欢白雪，所以今天下雪了，我真高兴！

_____

3) 因为天晴了，所以很多人在外面走路和跑步。

_____

4) 因为下大雨和刮大风，所以我不去商店了。

_____

5) 因为我很渴，所以我喝了很多水。

_____

4. Create your own sentences using the characters provided.

Example: 晴天：太好了，明天是晴天！

1) 阴天：_____

2) 下雨：_____

3) 下雪：_____

4) 很冷：_____

5) 很热：_____

6) 因为 ___ 所以 ___：_____

_____

5. Read the dialogues. Answer the questions using Chinese characters.

1) 小明：今天的天气怎么样？

    东东：今天是阴天。

    小明：你要去商店吗？

    东东：我不要去商店，我要去书店。

    Q1：今天天气怎么样？

    A1：_____

    Q2：东东要去哪儿？

    A2：_____

2) 小明：今天晚上很冷，你要去看电影吗？

    东东：这么冷，我不想去看电影，你呢？

    小明：你不去，我也不想去了。

    东东：我们在家看电视吧！

    Q1：他们为什么不去看电影？

    A1：_____

    Q2：他们在家做什么呢？

    A2：_____

3)　　小明：明天是晴天，我们去外面跑步，好吗？

　　　　东东：好啊！你想去哪里跑步？

　　　　小明：我想去那个公园。

　　　　东东：好，我们去公园跑步。

　　　　Q1：明天天气怎么样？

　　　　A1：＿＿＿＿＿＿＿＿＿＿＿＿＿＿＿＿

　　　　Q2：他们去哪儿跑步？

　　　　A2：＿＿＿＿＿＿＿＿＿＿＿＿＿＿＿＿

4)　　小明：外面下雨了，我们不去饭馆吃饭，好吗？

　　　　东东：雨下得很大吗？

　　　　小明：是的，雨下得很大。我们在家吃饭吧。

　　　　东东：好吧！我来做饭。

　　　　Q1：他们为什么不去饭馆了？

　　　　A1：＿＿＿＿＿＿＿＿＿＿＿＿＿＿＿＿

　　　　Q2：他们在那儿吃饭？

　　　　A2：＿＿＿＿＿＿＿＿＿＿＿＿＿＿＿＿

旅 (10 strokes)	**lǚ** travel, trip	**common words** 旅伴　**lǚbàn**　travel companion 旅馆　**lǚguǎn**　hotel; inn 旅游　**lǚyóu**　trip; journey; travel; tour	radical 方

汽 (7 strokes)	**qì** steam, vapor	**common words** 汽水　**qìshuǐ**　soda; pop 汽船　**qìchuán**　steamboat; steamship 公共汽车　**gōnggòng qìchē**　public bus	radical 氵

自 (6 strokes)	**zì** oneself, from, since	**common words** 自己　**zìjǐ**　oneself 自然　**zìrán**　nature 自行车　**zìxíngchē**　bicycle; bike	radical 自

船

chuán
boat,
ship

(11 strokes)

common words

船票　**chuánpiào**　ship ticket
船队　**chuánduì**　fleet of ships
船长　**chuánzhǎng**　captain of a ship; skipper

radical
舟

远

yuǎn
distant,
far,
remote

(7 strokes)

遠
Traditional

common words

远大　**yuǎndà**　far-reaching; broad
远见　**yuǎnjiàn**　vision
远走高飞　**yuǎnzǒu gāofēi**　to go far; to
escape to faraway places

radical
辶

近

jìn
near,
close to

(7 strokes)

common words

近视　**jìnshì**　nearsighted; myopia
近来　**jìnlái**　lately; recently
近水楼台　**jìnshuǐ lóutái**　(fig.) using one's
proximity to the powerful to obtain favor

radical
辶

70

| 慢 (14 strokes) | **màn** slow | **common words** 慢走　**mànzǒu**　(lit.) walk slowly; (fig.) wait a minute; take care 慢性　**mànxìng**　slow and patient; chronic (disease) 慢条斯理　**màntiáo sīlǐ**　slow and deliberate | radical 忄 |

忄　忄　忄　忄　忄　慢　慢　慢　慢　慢　慢

慢　慢　慢　慢　慢　慢

| 长 (4 strokes) | **cháng** long, always **zhǎng** grow 長 Traditional | **common words** 长寿　**chángshòu**　longevity; long life 长高了　**zhǎnggǎole**　grown taller 长话短说　**cháng huà duǎn shuō**　(idiom) to make a long story short | radical 长 |

长　长　长　长　长　长

| 等 (12 strokes) | **děng** to wait for, equal to, same as, class | **common words** 等于　**děngyú**　equal to 等级　**děngjí**　grade; rank; status 等而下之　**děng ér xià zhī**　(idiom) going from there to lower grades | radical 竹 |

等　等　等　等　等　等　等　等　等　等　等

等　等　等　等

从 (4 strokes)

cóng
from,
to obey

從
Traditional

radical
人

common words

自从　**zìcóng**　since; ever since
从事　**cóngshì**　to go for; to engage in
从容不迫　**cóngróng bú pò**　calm; unruffled

到 (8 strokes)

dào
to (a place),
up to,
to arrive

radical
刂

common words

到达　**dàodá**　to arrive; to reach
到处　**dàochù**　everywhere
到来　**dàolái**　advent; arrival

场 (6 strokes)

chǎng
field,
place,
scene
(of a play)

場
Traditional

radical
土

common words

场所　**chǎngsuǒ**　place; location
机场　**jīchǎng**　airport; airfield
广场　**guǎngchǎng**　public square; plaza

离 (10 strokes)	**lí** to leave, depart 離 **Traditional**	**common words** 离开 **líkāi** to leave; to depart 离婚 **líhūn** to divorce; divorced from 离乡背井 **líxiāng bèijǐng** (idiom) to live far from home; away from one's native place	**radical** 亠

丶 亠 六 文 这 㐄 㐄 离 离 离 离

离 离

比 (4 strokes)	**bǐ** to compare, ratio	**common words** 比方 **bǐfāng** analogy; for instance 比较 **bǐjiào** to compare; comparison 比比皆是 **bǐ bǐ jiē shì** can be found everywhere	**radical** 比

一 上 比 比 比 比 比

WORD PRACTICE

旅游 **lǚyóu**   trip, journey, travel, tour

旅	游							

公共汽车   **gōnggòng qìchē**   public bus

公	共	汽	车				

自行车   **zìxíngchē**   bicycle, bike

自	行	车			

机场   **jīchǎng**   airport, airfield

机	场						

时间   **shíjiān**   time

时	间						

小时   **xiǎoshí**   hour

小	时						

去年 **qùnián** last year

去	年								

EXERCISE SET 8 • 练习八
Where are You Going? • 你去哪儿?

---

1. **Match the English words with their Chinese counterparts:**

   Example: 1) – C.

   1) 旅游   2) 自行车   3) 船   4) 火车   5) 火车站

   6) 飞机   7) 飞机场   8) 出租车   9) 汽车   10) 公共汽车

   11) 快   12) 慢   13) 远   14) 近   15) 等

   A. air plane   B. boat   C. travel   D. bicycle   E. public bus
   F. train   G. car   H. taxi   I. train station J. airport
   K. wait   M. fast   N. slow   O. close   P. far

2. **Fill in the blanks using Chinese characters according to the pinyin.**

   1) 你坐 _____ (chūzūchē) 去哪里?

   2) 我会坐飞机去北京, 因为坐 _____ (fēijī) 比坐 _____ (huǒchē) 快很多。

   3) 这儿离 _____ (huǒchē zhàn) 很 _____ (jìn)。

   4) 您 _____ (màn) 点儿走, 我在这里 _____ (děngzhē) 您。

5) 我坐 _____ (gōnggòng qìchē) 去公园。

6) 你会开车吗？我不会 _____ (kāichē)。

3. These homophones have different meanings and usages. Rewrite them in the space provided.

飞(fēi) ←——→ 非(fēi) _____, _____

机(jī) ←——→ 鸡(jī) _____, _____

坐(zuò) ←——→ 做(zuò) _____, _____

玩(wán) ←——→ 完(wán) _____, _____

在(zài) ←——→ 再(zài) _____, _____

4. Make your own sentences using the characters provided.

Example: 很快：我们很快就要到家了！

1) 慢点儿：_____

2) 非常远：_____

3) 很近 ：_____

5. Read the dialogues. Answer the questions using Chinese characters.

1) 小明：你要去哪里旅游？

东东：我要去北京。

小明：你在北京玩多长时间？

东东：我在北京玩一个星期。

Q 1:　东东要去哪里？

A 1:　_____

Q 2:　东东在北京玩多长时间？

A 2:　_____

2)　小明：我明天要去外地开会。

东东：你怎么去？坐火车还是坐飞机？

小明：我坐飞机去。

东东：是啊，坐飞机比坐火车快。

Q 1:　小明要去哪里开会？

A 1:　_____

Q 2:　小明为什么坐飞机去开会？

A 2:　_____

3)　小明：你家离火车站有多远？

东东：很近，我走十五分钟，就到了。

东东：小明，你呢？

小明：我家比你家离火车站远，我要走一个多小时。

Q 1: 东东走到火车站，要多长时间？

A 1:　_____

Q 2:　小明走到火车站，要多长时间？

A 2:　_____

4) 小明：你怎么去商店？

   东东：我坐公共汽车去。

   小明：你怎么不开车去？

   东东：我不会开车。

   Q 1: 东东怎么去商店？

   A 1: _____

   Q 2: 东东为什么不开车去商店？

   A 2: _____

6. Translate these English sentences into Chinese.

1) How far from your home to the hospital?

   _____

2) How do you get into the airport?

   _____

3) Do you like to take train or airplane?

   _____

4) Please wait a few minutes for me?

   _____

5) Have you been to China?

   _____

动	dòng move, happen, action 動 Traditional	common words 运动 **yùndòng** sports; exercise 动作 **dòngzuò** motion; movement 动人心弦 **dòngrén xīnxián** be deeply moved; touch one's feeling	radical 力
(6 strokes)			

一	二	云	云	丂	动	动	动	动		

泳	yǒng swim	common words 泳衣 **yǒngyī** swim suit; bathing suit 泳池 **yǒngchí** swimming pool 游泳 **yóuyǒng** swimming; to swim	radical 氵
(8 strokes)			

丶	冫	氵	氵	汀	汈	泳	泳	泳	泳	泳

踢	tī kick, play	common words 踢开 **tīkāi** to kick open 踢足球 **tīzúqiú** to play soccer 拳打脚踢 **quándǎ jiǎotī** (lit.) to punch and kick; to beat up	radical 足
(15 strokes)			

丨	口	口	甲	早	尸	正	趴	趴	踋	跟
跟	跞	踢	踢	踢	踢	踢				

79

球

qiú
ball,
globe

(11 strokes)

common words

球鞋　**qiúxié**　athletic shoes
球队　**qiúduì**　sports team
球场　**qiúchǎng**　stadium; field; sports ground

radical
王

三	三	开	王	王	圹	打	玝	球	球	球
球	球	球								

篮

lán
basket

籃
Traditional

(16 strokes)

common words

篮子　**lánzi**　basket
投篮　**tóulán**　to shoot for the basket (as in a basketball game)
打篮球　**dǎlánqiú**　to play basketball

radical
竹

ノ	广	炸	竹	竺	竺	竿	筌	筌	筌	篆
篆	篮	篮	篮	篮	篮	篮	篮			

跳

tiào
jump,
skip,
hop

(13 strokes)

common words

跳水　**tiàoshuǐ**　diving
跳舞　**tiàowǔ**　to dance
吓一跳　**xiàyītiào**　startled; to frighten

radical
足

丨	口	口	马	足	呈	足	趴	趴	趴	跳
跳	跳	跳	跳	跳						

| 唱
(11 strokes) | **chàng**
sing,
chant | **common words**
唱片　**chàngpiàn**　gramaphone record; LP
唱歌　**chànggē**　to sing a song
唱独角戏　**chàng dújiǎoxì**　(lit.) put on a one-
　　man show; (fig.) do things all by oneself | **radical**
口 |

丨	口	吕	叫	吗	唱	唱	唱	唱	唱	唱
唱	唱	唱								

| 就
(12 strokes) | **jiù**
only,
then | **common words**
就业　**jiùyè**　getting a job
就职　**jiùzhí**　to assume office
就地取材　**jiùdì qǔcái**　use local resources;
　　using materials at hand | **radical**
尤 |

丶	二	六	古	亡	亨	京	京	京	就	就
就	就	就	就							

| 让
(5 strokes) | **ràng**
permit,
allow,
yield

讓
Traditional | **common words**
让座　**ràngzuò**　to give up one's seat
让位　**ràngwèi**　to abdicate; to yield
容让　**róngràng**　to make a concession; to be
　　accommodating | **radical**
讠 |

丶	讠	计	让	让	让	让				

过	**guò** to cross, to pass, to go over 過 Traditional	**common words** 过去　**guòqù**　in the past; former 过程　**guòchéng**　process; course of events 过河拆桥　**guòhé chāiqiáo**　(idiom) to destroy the bridge after crossing the river	radical 辶
(6 strokes)			

一	寸	寸	寸	讨	过	过	过	过	

但	**dàn** but, however, yet	**common words** 但是　**dànshì**　but; however 但凡　**dànfán**　every single, as long as 但愿如此　**dànyuàn rúcǐ**　if only it were so; let's hope so	radical 亻
(7 strokes)			

丿	亻	亻	佀	佀	佀	但	但	但	

WORD PRACTICE

运动 **yùndòng**　sports, exercise

运	动								

游泳 **yóuyǒng**　swimming

游	泳								

踢足球 **tīzúqiú**　to play soccer

踢	足	球						

打篮球 **dǎlánqiú**　to play basketball

打	篮	球						

跳舞 **tiàowǔ**　to dance

跳	舞								

唱歌 **chànggē**　to sing a song

唱	歌								

但是 **dànshì** but, however

但	是								

一起 **yīqǐ** together, with

一	起								

EXERCISE SET 9 • 练习九
Let's Exercise • 让我们一起运动

1. Add Pinyin and English next to these Chinese characters.

Chinese Characters	Pinyin	English	Chinese Characters	Pinyin	English
走路			打球		
跑步			游泳		
踢足球			打篮球		
唱歌			跳舞		
过去			现在		

2. **These homophones have different meanings and usage. Rewrite them in the space provided.**

舞 (wǔ)　　午 (wǔ)　　_____, _____

歌 (gē)　　哥 (gē)　　_____, _____

在 (zài)　　再 (zài)　　_____, _____

泳 (yǒng)　　永 (yǒng)　　_____, _____

球 (qiú)　　求 (qiú)　　_____, _____

3. **Identify the characters with the same radicals. Then write the characters in the space provided.**

路	游	送	跳	唱	汽
边	吃	跑	叫	没	远
泳	近	漂	过	踢	喝

足: _____, _____, _____, _____,

氵: _____, _____, _____, _____, _____,

辶: _____, _____, _____, _____, _____,

口: _____, _____, _____, _____,

4. Make your own sentences using the characters provided.

Example: 运动: 我们全家人都很喜欢运动。

1) 打球 : _____

2) 唱歌 : _____

3) 跳舞 : _____

4) 走路 : _____

5) 踢足球 : _____

6) 打篮球 : _____

5. Read the paragraph. Answers the question using Chinese characters.

A. 今天是晴天，不冷也不热，小明和他的美国朋友大为开车到公园里去玩。在公园里，他们看到很多人在运动。有的人在跑步，有的人在打篮球，有的人在踢足球，还有很多人在那里唱歌和跳舞。小明告诉大为，在中国，很多人喜欢在公园里唱唱歌，跳跳舞，他们觉得这样唱歌和跳舞，很开心。所以，他们会经常在公园里一起唱歌和跳舞。在美国，常常看到人们在公园里运动，但是，很少有人在那里唱歌和跳舞。

1) 今天天气怎么样？

_____

2) 人们在公园里做什么？

_____

3) 为什么很多中国人在公园里唱歌和跳舞？

_____

_____

4) 在美国的公园里，人们喜欢做什么？

_____

B. 小明和大为都非常喜欢运动。他们经常在一起打球。小明最喜欢打篮球，大为最喜欢踢足球。他们也很喜欢走路，跑步和游泳。每天下午，他们都会到球场去打篮球和踢足球。星期六和星期天，他们很喜欢到公园里去跑步。他们也常常去游泳馆去游泳。但是，他们没有在公园里唱歌和跳舞。

1) 小明最喜欢什么运动？

_____

2) 大为最喜欢什么运动？

_____

3) 星期六和星期天，他们很喜欢做什么？

_____

_____

4) 他们在公园里唱歌和跳舞吗？

_____

新	**xīn** new, recent, modern **(13 strokes)**	**common words** 新年　**xīnnián**　New Year 新潮　**xīncháo**　fashionable; modern 新来乍到　**xīnlái zhàdào**　newly arrived	**radical** 斤

丶	二	六	立	立	立	辛	辛	亲	亲	新
新	新	新	新	新						

手	**shǒu** hand **(4 strokes)**	**common words** 手册　**shǒucè**　handbook; manual 手机　**shǒujī**　cell phone; mobile phone 手无寸铁　**shǒu wú cùn tiě**　(lit.) not an inch of steel; unarmed and defenceless	**radical** 手

一	二	三	手	手	手	手				

表	**biǎo** wrist or pocket watch, surface **(8 strokes)**	**common words** 手表　**shǒubiǎo**　wrist watch 表演　**biǎoyǎn**　play; show; performance 表里如一　**biǎolǐ rúyī**　think and act as one; to say what one means	**radical** 衣

一	二	丰	圭	耒	表	表	表	表	表	表

两	**liǎng** two, both, some 兩 Traditional	**common words** 两手 **liǎngshǒu** double tactics; twin strategies 两面 **liǎngmiàn** both sides 两袖清风 **liǎngxiù qīngfēng** (idiom) both sleeves flowing in the wind; uncorrupted	**radical** 一

(7 strokes)

一	厂	币	丙	丙	两	两	两	两	两

百	**bǎi** hundred, numerous	**common words** 百年 **bǎinián** hundred years; century 百货 **bǎihuò** general merchandise 百读不厌 **bǎidú búyàn** (idiom) worth reading a hundred times	**radical** 白

(6 strokes)

一	丆	丆	百	百	百	百	百	百	

千	**qiān** thousand	**common words** 千米 **qiānmǐ** kilometer 千万 **qiānwàn** ten million; countless 千真万确 **qiānzhēn wànquè** absolutely true	**radical** 十

(3 strokes)

千	二	千	千	千	千				

元	**yuán** China currency	common words
(4 strokes)		元音　**yuányīn**　vowel 元旦　**yuándàn**　New Year's Day 元素周期表　**yuánsù zhōuqībiǎo**　periodic 　table of elements (chemistry)

radical 元

一	二	元	元	元	元	元					

便	**pián/biàn** cheap, convenient	common words
(9 strokes)		便宜　**piányí**　cheap; inexpensive 方便　**fāngbiàn**　convenient 大腹便便　**dàfù biànbiàn**　big-bellied; 　paunchy

radical 亻

丿	亻	亻	仁	�	伯	伊	便	便	便		
便											

第	**dì** prefix indicating number	common words
(11 strokes)		第一　**dìyī**　first; number one; primarily 第三者　**dìsānzhě**　the other man (woman); 　third party (in a dispute) 品第　**pǐndì**　grade (quality); rank

radical 竹

丿	仁	乍	灯	竹	竺	笃	笞	笃	第	第	
第	第	第									

次	cì number of times, order, secondary	**common words**		radical 冫
(6 strokes)		次数　**cìshù**　frequency; number of times 次要　**cìyào**　secondary 次之　**cìzhī**　occupying second place		

次	冫	丬	汃	次	次	次	次	次		

斤	jīn unit of weight, catty (unit in weight)	**common words**		radical 斤
(4 strokes)		斤两　**jīnliǎng**　weight; (fig.) importance 公斤　**gōngjīn**　kilogram 斤斤计较　**jīnjīn jìjiào**　haggle over every 　　ounce; (fig.) to fuss over minor matters		

一	厂	斤	斤	斤	斤	斤				

卖	mài to sell, to betray 賣 Traditional	**common words**		radical 十
(8 strokes)		卖力　**màilì**　to really put out energy for 卖国　**màiguó**　to sell one's country; treason 卖关子　**màiguānzi**　to keep the listeners in 　　suspense (in storytelling); to keep people on 　　tenterhooks		

一	十	士	声	声	壶	卖	卖	卖	卖	卖

WORD PRACTICE

手机　**shǒujī**　cell phone, mobile phone

手	机						

手表　**shǒubiǎo**　wrist watch

手	表						

便宜　**piányí**　cheap

便	宜						

第一　**dìyī**　first, number one, primarily

第	一						

公斤　**gōngjīn**　kilogram

公	斤						

1. **Read these words. Each character has two different meanings. Copy the Chinese characters in the space provided.**

便 (pián)　　便 (pián) 宜(yí) / cheap　　　_____

便

便 (biàn)　　方 (fāng) 便 (biàn) / convenient　　_____

觉 (jiào)　　睡 (shuì) 觉 (jiào) / sleep　　　_____

觉

觉 (jué)　　觉 (jué) 得 (de) / feel　　　_____

乐 (lè)　　快 (kuài) 乐 (lè) / happy　　　_____

乐

乐 (yuè)　　音 (yīn) 乐 (yuè) / music　　　_____

行 (xíng)　　自 (zì) 行 (xíng) 车 (chē) / bicycle_____

行

行 (háng)　　银 (yín) 行 (háng) / bank　　　_____

长 →
长 (cháng)　很 (hěn) 长 (cháng) / very long　　_____

长 (zhǎng)　长 (zhǎng) 大 (dà) / grow up　　_____

2. Add the Pinyin and English next to the Chinese characters.

Chinese Characters	Pinyin	English	Chinese Characters	Pinyin	English
手表			一千元		
手机			一千块		
便宜			两百元		
很贵			两百块		
公斤			第一		
几公斤			第一次		

3. Make your own sentences using the characters provided.

Example: 买：　爸爸给我买了一个新手机。

1)　卖　　：　_____

2)　便宜　：　_____

3)　太贵了：　_____

94

4. Read the dialogues. Answers the questions using Chinese characters.

1) 小明： 请问，这件衣服，要多少钱？

　　卖主： 这件衣服要 50 块钱。

　　小明： 有蓝颜色的吗？

　　卖主： 有。

　　小明： 我买一件蓝色的衣服。

　　Q 1： 那件衣服要多少钱？

　　A 1： ＿＿＿＿＿＿＿＿＿＿＿＿＿＿＿＿＿＿＿＿

　　Q 2： 小明买了一件什么颜色的衣服？

　　A 2： ＿＿＿＿＿＿＿＿＿＿＿＿＿＿＿＿＿＿＿＿

2) 东东： 请问，苹果怎么卖？

　　卖主： 三块八一斤。

　　东东： 太贵了！便宜点儿，行吗？

　　卖主： 三块三，怎么样？

　　东东： 好的，我买四斤。

　　Q 1： 东东买了几斤苹果？

　　A 1： ＿＿＿＿＿＿＿＿＿＿＿＿＿＿＿＿＿＿＿＿

　　Q 2： 东东买的苹果是多少钱一斤？

　　A 2： ＿＿＿＿＿＿＿＿＿＿＿＿＿＿＿＿＿＿＿＿

3) 大为：请问，这本中文书要多少钱？

卖主：这本书要一块五。

大为：那本书呢？

卖主：那本要两块三。

大为：好的，这两本书，我都买了，给你三块八。

卖主：谢谢！

Q 1: 大为买了几本书？

A 1: _____

Q 2: 两本书一共要多少钱？

A 2: _____

4) 小明：这张桌子，怎么卖？

卖主：要五百九十块钱。

小明：那把椅子呢？

卖主：那把椅子要一百九十块钱。

小明：我要买一张桌子，四把椅子，一共要多少钱？

卖主：一共要一千三百五十块钱。

小明：好的，这是一千三百五十块钱。

卖主：谢谢！

Q 1: 一张桌子要多少钱？

A 1: _____

Q 2: 一把椅子要多少钱？

A 2: _____

Q 3: 小明买了一张桌子和四把椅子，一共用了多少钱？

A 3: _____

每	**měi** every, each	**common words** 每天　**měitiān**　every day 每月　**měiyuè**　each month 每况愈下　**měi kuàng yù xià**　to steadily 　deteriorate; to go from bad to worse	**radical** 母
(7 strokes)			

ノ	←	←	勹	勹	每	每	每	每	每

早	**zǎo** morning, early	**common words** 早安　**zǎoān**　Good morning! 早上　**zǎoshàng**　early morning 早晚　**zǎowǎn**　(lit.) morning and evening; 　(fig.) sooner or later	**radical** 日
(6 strokes)			

ノ	日	日	旦	旦	早	早	早	早	

晚	**wǎn** late, evening, night	**common words** 晚辈　**wǎnbèi**　the younger generation 晚上　**wǎnshàng**　evening; night 一天到晚　**yītiān dào wǎn**　all day long	**radical** 日
(11 strokes)			

∣	∏	日	日	日′	日″	晚	晚	晚	晚	晚
晚	晚	晚								

床	**chuáng**	**common words**	radical
(7 strokes)	bed, couch	床单　**chuángdān**　bed sheet 起床　**qǐchuáng**　to get out of bed 床第之言　**chuángdì zhīyán**　pillow talk; intimate conversation between husband and wife	广

床 广 庁 庁 床 床 床 床

洗	**xǐ**	**common words**	radical
(9 strokes)	to wash, to bathe	洗手　**xǐshǒu**　to wash one's hands 洗钱　**xǐqián**　money laundering 洗耳恭听　**xǐěr gōngtīng**　listen with respectful attention; (idiom) I am all ears!	氵

洗 洗 氵 氵 汗 汼 洗 涉 洗 洗 洗
洗

报	**bào**	**common words**	radical
(7 strokes)	report, inform, newspaper	报告　**bàogào**　inform; report; make known 报纸　**bàozhǐ**　newspaper 报喜不报忧　**bàoxǐ bù bàoyōu**　report only the good news; hold back unpleasant news	扌

一 扌 扌 扪 护 报 报 报 报

司	**sī** to manage, department (under a ministry)	**common words** 司机 **sījī** chauffer; driver 公司 **gōngsī** company; firm; corportion 司空见惯 **sīkōng jiànguàn** (idiom) a common occurrence	**radical** 丁

(5 strokes)

司 司 司 司 司 司 司

班	**bān** class, team, work shift	**common words** 班车 **bānchē** regular bus (service) 上班 **shàngbān** to go to work; to be on duty 班门弄斧 **bānmén nòngfǔ** (idiom) to display one's slight skill before an expert	**radical** 王

(10 strokes)

一 二 于 王 玡 玥 班 班 班 班

班 班

事	**shì** matter, thing, item, work	**common words** 事实 **shìshí** fact 事情 **shìqíng** affair; matter; business 事半功倍 **shìbàn gōngbèi** (lit.) half the work, twice the effect; the right effort leads to better results	**radical** 一

(8 strokes)

一 丆 丆 軎 寻 寻 事 事 事 事

票	piào	common words	radical
(11 strokes)	ticket, ballot, banknote	票价　**piàojià**　ticket price; admission fee 票箱　**piàoxiāng**　ballot box 支票　**zhīpiào**　check (bank)	示

一	一	帀	帀	襾	西	覀	覀	覀	票	票

票	票	票								

意	yì	common words	radical
(13 strokes)	meaning, idea, thought, wish	意见　**yìjiàn**　opinion; idea 意思　**yìsi**　meaning; desire 意味深长　**yìwèi shēncháng**　full of meaning; 　　eloquent; significant	心

丶	二	亠	立	立	音	音	音	音	音	意

意	意	意	意	意						

WORD PRACTICE

早上 **zǎoshàng** early morning

早	上							

晚上 **wǎnshàng** evening, night

晚	上							

起床 **qǐchuáng** to get out of bed

起	床							

公司 **gōngsī** company, firm, corporation

公	司							

上班 **shàngbān** to go to work; to be on duty

上	班							

事情 **shìqíng** affair, matter, business

事	情							

报纸 **bàozhǐ** newspaper

报	纸							

意思 **yìsi** meaning, wish, desire

意	思							

EXERCISE SET 11 • 练习十一
One of My Days • 我的一天

1. Match the Chinese vocabulary with their English counterparts.

A. 早上　　　B. 晚上　　　C. 起床　　　D. 报纸

E. 公司　　　F. 上班　　　G. 事情　　　H. 意思

1. company　　2. get up　　3. go to work　　4. newspaper

5. night　　6. meaning　　7. morning　　8. things

2. Read the questions. Rewrite the answers in Chinese characters.

Q1: 你早上几点起床？

A1:　I get up at six o'clock.

Q2: 你早上几点吃早饭？

A2: I eat breakfast at six thirty.

Q3: 你几点上班？

A3: I go to work at eight o'clock.

Q4: 你几点吃午饭？

A4: I eat lunch at twelve o'clock.

Q5: 你几点下班？

A5: I get out work at five o'clock afternoon.

Q6: 你几点吃晚饭？

A6: I eat dinner at seven o'clock.

Q7: 你几点睡觉？

A7: I go to bed at ten o'clock.

---

3. Make your own sentences using the characters provided.

Example: 起床： 妹妹每天早上六点半起床。

1) 上班 ： _____

2) 吃晚饭 ： _____

3) 睡觉 ： _____

4) 做事情 ： _____

4. Choose the accurate words from the word-bank. Write them in the space provided.

起床	早上	咖啡	报纸	公司
早饭	上班	下班	七点五十分	电影票
午饭	吃晚饭	电影院	在家里	八点钟

我每天（   ）六点钟（   ），六点半吃（   ）。早上，我喜欢一边喝（   ），一边看（   ）。我七点二十分离开家，开车去（   ）。我路上要开半个小时，经常是在（   ）到公司门口。我们（   ）是早上（   ）上班，下午五点钟（   ）。我中午在公司的咖啡厅里吃（   ）。每天下班后，我就回家。星期五和星期六的晚上，有时我会和朋友们一起去餐馆（   ），有时我们会到（   ）里看电影。晚上的电影票比白天的（   ）要贵一点。当天气不好的时候，我就（   ）看电视，哪里也不去了。

5. Read the paragraph. Answer the question in Chinese.

A.   小英每天早上六点半起床，她七点钟吃早饭。早饭后，她骑自行车去上学。因为小英的家离学校很近，她骑车十分钟就到了，所以她每天骑车上学。小英下午三点二十分放学。放学后，她在学校打篮球。打完球后，她回家吃晚饭。晚饭后，她会做作业。她晚上九点钟睡觉。

1)   小英每天几点起床？几点吃早饭？

_____

_____

2)   小英怎么去上学？

_____

3)   小英下午几点放学？

_____

4)   放学后，小英做什么？

_____

_____

5)   小英晚上几点睡觉？

_____

B.   小红每天早上五点钟半起床后，要给全家人做早饭。早饭后，她先生去医院上班，她去飞机场上班。他们的儿子和女儿坐校车去上学。上班时，小红每天都很忙，有很多事情要做。但是，她很喜欢她的工作，因为她觉得能够帮助别人是她最大的快乐。下班后，有时小红做晚饭，有时她先生做晚饭。晚饭后，孩子们做功课，小红和先生会看看书和报纸。他们的孩子每天晚上九点钟睡觉。小红和先生十点钟睡觉。

1) 小红每天早上几点起床？

_____

2) 小红的先生在哪里工作？小红呢？

_____

_____

3) 小红为什么很喜欢她的工作？

_____

_____

4) 小红的孩子们怎么去上学？

_____

5) 在小红的家里，谁做早饭？谁做晚饭？

_____

_____

6) 晚饭后，他们做什么？

_____

_____

7) 小红的孩子们几点睡觉？

_____

8) 小红和她先生几点睡觉？

_____

身	**shēn** body, oneself, personally	**common words**	
(7 strokes)		身体　**shēntǐ**　the body; one's health 身教　**shēnjiào**　to teach by example 身外之物　**shēnwài zhī wù**　external things 　　not physically connected to oneself	**radical** 身

ノ	イ	白	白	身	身	身	身	身	身

眼	**yǎn** eye, small hole	**common words**	
(11 strokes)		眼镜　**yǎnjìng**　eyeglasses; spectacles 眼睛　**yǎnjīng**　eye 眼高手低　**yǎn gāoshǒu dī**　have high 　　standards but little ability	**radical** 目

丨	刀	月	目	目	目	目	目	眼	眼	眼
眼	眼	眼								

累	**lèi** tired **lěi** accumulate	**common words**	
(11 strokes)		累坏　**lèihuài**　to become exhausted 累计　**lěijì**　to accumulate 日积月累　**rìjī yuèlěi**　to accumulate over a 　　long period of time	**radical** 糸

ノ	口	曰	田	田	累	累	累	累	累	累
累	累	累								

| 忙 (6 strokes) | **máng** busy | **common words** 忙乱　**mángluàn**　rushed and muddled
 帮忙　**bāngmáng**　to help
 忙忙叨叨　**mángmáng dāodāo**　in a busy and hasty manner | **radical** 忄 |

| 忄 | 忄 | 忄 | 忄 | 忙 | 忙 | 忙 | 忙 | 忙 |

| 病 (10 strokes) | **bìng** disease, illness, to fall ill | **common words** 生病　**shēngbìng**　to fall ill
 病因　**bìngyīn**　cause of disease
 病入膏肓　**bìng rù gāohuāng**　(lit.) the disease has attacked the vitals; (fig.) beyond cure | **radical** 疒 |

| 丶 | 二 | 广 | 疒 | 疒 | 疒 | 疒 | 病 | 病 | 病 | 病 |
| 病 | 病 | | | | | | | | | |

| 药 (9 strokes) | **yào** medicine 藥 **Traditional** | **common words** 药方　**yàofāng**　prescription
 药房　**yàofáng**　pharmacy; drugstore
 药到病除　**yào dào bìng chú**　as the medicine took effect the symptoms lessened | **radical** 艹 |

| 一 | 十 | 艹 | 艹 | 艻 | 艻 | 药 | 药 | 药 | 药 |
| 药 | | | | | | | | | |

| 休 (6 strokes) | **xiū** to rest, to cease | **common words** 休息　**xiūxī**　rest; take a break 休想　**xiūxiǎng**　don't think (that) 休戚与共　**xiū qī yǔ gòng**　stand together through thick and thin | **radical** 亻 |

| 望 (11 strokes) | **wàng** to hope, to look towards, expect | **common words** 希望　**xīwàng**　to wish for; to desire; hope 望月　**wàngyuè**　full moon 望尘莫及　**wàngchén mòjí**　too far behind to catch up; too inferior to bear comparison | **radical** 王 |

| 别 (7 strokes) | **bié** separate, other, do not | **common words** 别人　**biérén**　other people 别说　**biéshuō**　needless to say; let alone 别开生面　**bié kāi shēng miàn**　(idiom) to start something new; to break fresh ground | **radical** 刂 |

WORD PRACTICE

身体　**shēntǐ**　the body, one's health

身	体								

眼睛　**yǎnjīng**　eye

眼	睛								

生病　**shēngbìng**　to fall ill

生	病								

休息　**xiūxī**　rest, take a break

休	息								

希望　**xīwàng**　to wish for, to desire, hope

希	望								

1. **Add the Pinyin and English next to these Chinese characters.**

Chinese Characters	Pinyin	English	Chinese Characters	Pinyin	English
身体			很累		
眼睛			很忙		
生病			希望		
吃药			休息		

2. **Read and rewrite these phrases in Chinese characters.**

别太累了 （　　　　　　）　　别再说了 （　　　　　　　　　）

别再忙了 （　　　　　　）　　别再写了 （　　　　　　　　　）

别再看了 （　　　　　　）　　别再做了 （　　　　　　　　　）

别再走了 （　　　　　　）　　别再跑了 （　　　　　　　　　）

3. **Read the dialogues. Answer the question using Chinese characters.**

1) 妈妈: 东东, 别再看电脑了！

   东东: 好的。

   妈妈: 你知道, 看电脑时间长了, 眼睛会很累。

   东东: 我知道, 我这就不看了。

Q 1:　妈妈对东东说什么？

A 1:　_____

Q 2:　东东为什么不再看电脑了？

A 2:　_____

　　　_____

2)　妈妈：东东，你今天怎么了？

　　东东：我可能生病了。

　　妈妈：你要去看一下医生。

　　东东：我会的，谢谢！

Q 1:　东东怎么了？

A 1:　_____

Q 2:　妈妈对东东说什么？

A 2:　_____

3)　妈妈：东东，你好像很累，是吗？

　　东东：是的，我这几天工作很忙，也很累。

　　妈妈：你要好好地休息一下。

　　东东：谢谢！我会的。

Q 1:　东东这几天怎么了？

A 1:　_____

　　　_____

Q 2:　妈妈要东东做什么？

A 2:　_____

_____

4)　东东：妈妈，你去看医生了吗？

妈妈：去了。医生说，不是大问题，吃两天药就会好。

东东：那您吃药了吗？

妈妈：我吃过药了。

Q 1:　医生对妈妈说了什么？

A 1:　_____

_____

Q 2:　妈妈吃药了吗？

A 2:　_____

5)　东东：妈妈，我们出去走路，好吗？

妈妈：好的，每天走路，身体好。

东东：那以后我们每天走路半个小时，怎么样？

妈妈：没问题！

Q 1:　东东要和妈妈做什么？为什么？

A 1:　_____

_____

Q 2:　他们每天要走多长时间？

A 2:　_____

4. Make your own sentences using the characters provided.

Example: 休息：小明工作很忙，每天都到很晚才休息。

1)　吃药：_____

2)　很忙：_____

3)　很累：_____

4)　希望：_____

5. Read the paragraph. Answers the questions using Chinese characters.

现在，你常听到人们说"我工作很忙，没时间运动"；
"我太忙了，没时间打球"；"我一天忙到晚，我很
累"⋯⋯大为以前也是这样，但是从今年起，他每天下班
后，跑步一个小时。星期六和星期天的下午，他还要去球
场打一个小时的篮球，再游泳一个小时。小明和东东也要
在新的一年里，每天都要走路，跑步和游泳。他们都希望
自己能有一个好身体，少生病，少去医院。他们都知道只
有身体好，才能很好地工作和学习，也才能快乐地生活。

Q 1:　现在，你常听到人们说什么？

A 1:　_____

_____

_____

Q 2: 大为今年要做什么？

A 2: _____

_____

Q 3: 星期六和星期天下午，大为做什么？

A 3: _____

_____

_____

Q 4: 新的一年里，小明和东东要做什么？

A 4: _____

_____

_____

Q 5: 为什么他们都要去运动？

A 5: _____

_____

_____

Answer Key

Exercise Set 1

1.1　1) 开始　2) 欢迎　3) 大家　4) 贵姓　5) 介绍　6) 快乐

1.2　辶: 送, 迎, 这; 纟: 绍, 给; 日: 最, 星; 女: 姓, 始, 她

1.3　1) 小明的生日是十月六号, 星期五。

2) 小明最喜欢的书。

3) 东东要去中国学中文, 明年。

4) 因为是小明的生日。

Exercise Set 2

2.1　丈夫—zhàngfū—husband; 妻子—qīzi—wife; 男人—nánrén—men, male;

女人—nǚrén—woman, female; 哥哥—gēge—older brother; 弟弟—dìdi—younger brother;

姐姐—jiějie—older sister; 妹妹—mèimei—younger sister; 孩子—háizi—child, children;

房间—fángjiān—room

2.2　1) 常常, 电视, 电影　2) 北京　3) 在一起　4) 妻子　5) 丈夫　6) 玩笑

2.4　1) 李星的丈夫是医生。

2) 李星是老师。

3) 大儿子二十一岁, 上大学; 小儿子十七岁, 上高中。

4) 女儿十二岁, 上中学。

Exercise Set 3

3.1　鱼, 羊肉, 牛奶, 鸡蛋, 咖啡, 茶, 西瓜, 苹果

3.2　1) 羊肉, 牛肉　2) 鱼　3) 经常, 吃饭　4) 咖啡　5) 茶　6) 还要　7) 鸡蛋　8) 非常

3.4　1) 他们买了很多羊肉和牛肉。

2) 他们还买了鸡蛋, 牛奶和很多菜。

3) 那家咖啡店也卖茶。

4) 他们都非常喜欢吃西瓜和苹果。

3.6　星期天下午, 妈妈和我去（商店）买肉, 菜和水果。我们买了（羊）肉, （牛）肉,
（鸡）蛋和鱼。我们（也买了）很多菜和牛（奶）。我们还（买了）苹果
和（西瓜）。买完（东西）, 妈妈和我去了一家咖啡店。这家（咖啡店）的咖啡和
茶都很好。妈妈要了一杯咖啡, 我要了（一杯）茶。妈妈说她的（咖啡）很好喝,
我的（茶）也很好喝。我们都（非常）喜欢这家咖啡店, 下次我们（还会去）这家
咖啡店喝咖啡和茶。

Exercise Set 4

4.1　字—zì—character; 子—zǐ—seed, son; 们—men—use as a person to form a plural; 门—mén—door; 没—méi—don't have; 妹—mèi—younger sister; 羊—yáng—lamb; 样—yàng—sample; 完—wán—finish; 玩—wán—play; 非—fēi—not, non, negative; 飞—fēi—fly; 买—mǎi—to buy; 卖—mài—to sell; 前—qián—front; 钱—qián—money; 机—jī—machine; 鸡—jī—chicken; 那—nà—that; 哪—nǎ—where.

4.2　1) 教室　2) 课　3) 回答　4) 帮助

4.4　1) 老师说得太快／他们去问老师。

2) 两个外国学生／他们的汉语很好。

3) 东东每天上五门课／一门课是四十五分钟。

4) 他们明天有三门考试／小明准备好了，东东没有／东东有一个问题不知道怎么回答／东东懂了。

Exercise Set 5

5.2　1) 商店在学校的左边。

2) 医院在商店的后面。

3) 火车站在医院的右边。

4) 是的，饭馆在商店的左边。

5) 外面的天气很好。

6) 妈妈的茶杯在桌子上。

7) 是的，教室里有很多学生。

8) 没有，商店前面只有几辆车。

5.4　1) 小明要去商店买东西。

2) 他打电话问他的朋友。

3) 火车站在商店的右边。

4) 医院在商店的左边。

5) 书店在商店的前面。

6) 电影院在商店的后面。

7) 小明买到了他想要的东西。

Exercise Set 6

6.1　颜色—yánsè—color; 白色—báisè—white color; 黑色—hēisè—black color; 红色—hóngsè—red color; 五颜六色—wǔyánliùsè—multi-color; 白色衣服—báisè yīfū—white color clothing

6.4　1) 我喜欢这件红衣服。

2) 你可以试一试那件白上衣。

3) 我们没有小一点的衣服。

4) 好吧，我买这件衣服。

5) 那个红色杯子是我的。

6) 这件黑色的衣服很漂亮。

7) 是的，我今天洗了衣服。

8) 我最喜欢红色。

6.6　1) 小明和东东去商店买衣服。

2) 小明很喜欢一件白色的上衣。

3) 商店里的衣服可以试穿。

4) 小明穿上正好，他就买了那件白上衣。

5) 东东喜欢那件红，黑和白三种颜色在一起的衣服。

6) 因为她穿上那件衣服很漂亮。

Exercise Set 7

7.1　晴—sunny—qíng; 阴 cloudy—yīn; 雨—rain—yǔ; 雪—snow-xuě; 风—wind—fēng;
冷—cold—lěng; 热—hot—rè

7.5　1) 今天是阴天。/ 东东要去书店。

2) 晚上很冷。/ 他们在家看电视。

3) 明天是晴天。/ 他们去公园跑步。

4) 外面下大雨了。/ 他们在家吃饭。

Exercise Set 8

8.1　1) C; 2) D; 3)-B; 4) F; 5) I; 6) A; 7) J; 8) H; 9) G; 10) E; 11) M; 12) N; 13) P; 14) O; 15) K

8.2　1) 出租车　2) 飞机/火车　3) 火车站 / 近　4) 慢/等着　5) 公共汽车　6) 开车

8.5　1) 东东要去北京。/ 东东在北京玩一个星期。

2) 小明要去外地开会 。/ 因为坐飞机比坐火车快。

3) 东东要走十五分钟。/ 小明要走一个多小时。

4) 东东坐公共汽车去商店。/ 因为东东不会开车。

8.6　1) 从你家到医院有多远？

2) 你怎么去机场？

3) 你喜欢坐火车还是飞机？

4) 请等我几分钟。

5) 你去过中国吗？

Exercise Set 9

9.1　走路—zǒulù—to walk; 打球—dǎqiú—to play ball; 跑步—pǎobù—to run;
游泳—yóuyǒng—to swim; 踢足球—tīzúqiú—to play soccer; 打篮球—dǎlánqiú—to play
basketball; 唱歌—chànggē—to sing a song; 跳舞—tiàowǔ—to dance; 过去—guòqù—past;
现在—xiànzài—now

9.3　足:路 / 跑 / 踢 / 跳; 氵:游 / 泳 / 漂 / 没 / 汽; 辶:过 / 远 / 近 / 运 / 边; 口:唱 / 吃 / 喝 / 叫

9.5　A. 1) 今天是晴天，不冷也不热。

2) 人们在公园里运动，跑步，打篮球，踢足球，唱歌和跳舞。

    3) 因为中国人觉得在公园里唱歌和跳舞，很开心。

    4) 美国人喜欢在公园里运动。

B. 1) 小明最喜欢打篮球。

    2) 大为最喜欢踢足球。

    3) 星期六和星期天，他们很喜欢到公园里去跑步和游泳。

    4) 他们没有在公园里唱歌和跳舞。

Exercise Set 10

10.2 手表—shǒubiǎo—watch; 手机—shǒujī—cell phone; 便宜—piányí—cheap; 很贵—hěnguì—very expensive; 公斤—gōngjīn—kilogram; 几公斤—jǐgōngjīn—how many kilogram; 一千元—yìqiānyuán—one thousand dollars; 一千块—yìqiānkuài—one thousand dollars; 两百元—liǎngbǎiyuán—two hundred dollars/两百块—liǎngbǎikuài—two hundred dollars/第一—dìyī—first, number one; 第一次—dìyīcì—first time

10.4 1) 那件衣服要 50 块钱。／小明买了一件蓝色的衣服。

2) 东东买了四斤苹果。／东东买的苹果是三块三一斤。

3) 大为买了两本书。／两本书要三块八。

4) 一张桌子要五百九十块钱。／一把椅子要一百九十块钱。／一共用了一千三百五十块钱。

Exercise Set 11

11.1 A-7; B-5; C-2; D-4; E-1; F-3; G-8; H-6

11.2 A. 1) 我早上六点起床。

    2) 我早上六点半吃早饭。

    3) 我八点上班。

    4) 我十二点吃午饭。

    5) 我下午五点下班。

    6) 我七点吃晚饭。

    7) 我十点睡觉。

11.4 我每天（早上）六点钟（起床），六点半吃（早饭）。早上，我喜欢一边喝（咖啡），一边看（报纸）。我七点二十分离开家，开车去（上班）。我路上要开半个小时，经常是在（七点五十分）到公司门口。我们（公司）是早上（八点钟）上班，下午五点钟（下班）。我中午在公司的咖啡厅里吃（午饭）。每天下班后，我就回家。星期五和星期六的晚上，有时候，我会和朋友们一起去餐馆（吃晚饭），有时我们会到（电影院）里看电影。晚上的电影票比白天的（电影票）要贵一点。当天气不好的时候，我就（在家里）看电视，哪里也不去了。

11.5 A. 1) 小英每天六点半起床，七点吃早饭。

    2) 小英骑自行车去上学。

    3) 小英下午三点二十分放学。

    4) 放学后，小英先在学校打篮球，然后回家吃晚饭和做作业。

5) 小英晚上九点睡觉。

B. 1) 小红每天早上五点半起床。

2) 小红的先生在医院工作，小红在飞机场工作。

3) 因为小红觉得能够帮助别人是最大的快乐。

4) 小红的孩子们坐校车去上学。

5) 在小红的家里，小红做早饭；有时小红做晚饭，有时她先生做晚饭。

6) 晚饭后，孩子们做功课，小红和先生会看看书和报纸。

7) 小红的孩子们九点睡觉。

8) 小红和她先生十点睡觉。

Exercise Set 12

12.1 身体—shēntǐ—the body; 眼睛—yǎnjīng—eye; 生病—shēngbìng—to fall ill; 吃药—chīyào—to take medicine; 很累—hěnlèi—very tired; 很忙—hěnmáng—very busy; 希望—xīwàng—to wish for, to desire, hope; 休息—xiūxī—rest, take a break

12.3 1) 妈妈说别再看电脑了！/ 因为看电脑时间长了，眼睛会很累。

2) 东东可能生病了。/ 妈妈要东东去看一下医生。

3) 东东这几天工作很忙，也很累。/ 妈妈要东东好好地休息一下。

4) 医生说，不是大问题，吃两天药就会好。/ 妈妈吃过药了。

5) 东东要和妈妈出去走路，因为每天走路身体好。/ 他们每天要走半个小时。

12.5 1）现在人们常说"我工作很忙，没时间运动"；"我太忙了，没时间打球"；"我一天忙到晚，我很累"。

2) 大为从今年起，每天下班后，跑步一小时。

3) 星期六和星期天的下午，大为要去球场打一个小时的篮球，再游泳一个小时。

4) 小明和东东也要在新的一年里，每天都要走路，跑步和游泳。

5) 他们都希望自己能有一个好身体。因为只有身体好，才能很好地工作和学习，也才能快乐地生活。

English–Chinese Index

A

a measure word for flat objects　张　**zhāng**　54
a measure word for things, item　件　**jiàn**　54
a particle indicating action in progress　着　**zhe**　55
a particle, bar　吧　**ba**　63
accumulate　累　**lěi**　108
affair, matter, business　事情　**shìqíng**　100
airport, airfield　机场　**jīchǎng**　72
allow, standard, accurate　备　**bèi**　38
already　已经　**yǐjīng**　28
already, then　已　**yǐ**　28
also, too, as well　也　**yě**　28
answer, respond, reply　答　**dá**　37
assist, help, gang　帮　**bāng**　39
attendant, customer service personnel　服务员　**fúwù yuán**　55

B

ball, globe　球　**qiú**　80
basket　篮　**lán**　80
because, owing to　因为　**yīnwèi**　62
because of, for, to　为　**wèi**　55
bed, couch　床　**chuáng**　99
begin, start　始　**shǐ**　12
beside, to the side　旁边　**pángbiān**　46
bike　自行车　**zìxíngchē**　69
birthday　生日　**shēngrì**　15
black (color), dark　黑　**hēi**　53
boat, ship　船　**chuán**　70
body, oneself　身　**shēn**　108
busy　忙　**máng**　109
but, however　但　**dàn**　82
but, however　但是　**dànshì**　82

C

can, may, possible　可以　**kěyǐ**　44
cause, reason　因　**yīn**　62
cell phone, mobile phone　手机　**shǒujī**　88
cheap　便宜　**piányí**　90
cheap, convenient　便　**pián/biàn**　90
chicken　鸡　**jī**　27
child　孩　**hái**　19
child, children　孩子　**háizi**　19
China currency　元　**yuán**　90
class, team, work shift　班　**bān**　100

(continued)

class, lesson, subject　课　**kè**　35
classroom　教室　**jiàoshì**　36
cloudy, shady　阴　**yīn**　61
coffee　咖　**kā**　27
coffee　咖啡　**kāfēi**　27
color, face　颜　**yán**　52
color　颜色　**yánsè**　52
company, firm, corporation　公司　**gōngsī**　100
cow　牛　**niú**　26
curry　咖　**gā**　27

D

disease, sickness　病　**bìng**　109
distant, far, remote　远　**yuǎn**　70
do not, other, separate　别　**bié**　110
door, gate　门　**mén**　35

E

early morning　早上　**zǎoshàng**　98
egg　鸡蛋　**jīdàn**　27
enter, advance　进　**jìn**　46
evening, night　晚上　**wǎnshàng**　98
every, each　每　**měi**　98
everyone, big family　大家　**dàjiā**　15
exam, to take an exam　考试　**kǎoshì**　36
expensive, precious　贵　**guì**　14
eye　眼　**yǎn**　108
eye　眼睛　**yǎnjīng**　108

F

family name　姓　**xìng**　14
fast, quickly, hurry up　快　**kuài**　11
field, place, scene (of a play)　场　**chǎng**　72
finish, whole, complete　完　**wán**　29
first, primarily, number one　第一　**dìyī**　90
fish　鱼　**yú**　26
from, to obey　从　**cóng**　72

G

gain, get, obtain　得　**dé**　53
get up, wake up　起床　**qǐchuáng**　99
give, by, for　给　**gěi**　13
greet, welcome　迎　**yíng**　12
grow　长　**zhǎng**　71

Hanyu Pinyin Index

About Tuttle
"Books to Span the East and West"

Our core mission at Tuttle Publishing is to create books which bring people together one page at a time. Tuttle was founded in 1832 in the small New England town of Rutland, Vermont (USA). Our fundamental values remain as strong today as they were then—to publish best-in-class books informing the English-speaking world about the countries and peoples of Asia. The world has become a smaller place today and Asia's economic, cultural and political influence has expanded, yet the need for meaningful dialogue and information about this diverse region has never been greater. Since 1948, Tuttle has been a leader in publishing books on the cultures, arts, cuisines, languages and literatures of Asia. Our authors and photographers have won numerous awards and Tuttle has published thousands of books on subjects ranging from martial arts to paper crafts. We welcome you to explore the wealth of information available on Asia at **www.tuttlepublishing.com.**